People and Politics:

An Introduction to American Government Study Guide

Fourteenth Edition

People and Politics:

An Introduction to American Government Study Guide

Fourteenth Edition

Mary Kate Hiatt
Delta College
University Center, Michigan

Gregory Publishing Company   Wheaton, IL 60189

Design and Production: Gregory Publishing Company
Typeface: AGaramond
Typesetting: Gregory Publishing Company
Cover Art: Sam Tolia

People and Politics:
An Introduction to American Government Study Guide

Fourteenth Edition, 2009
Printed in the United States of America
Translation rights reserved by the authors
ISBN 0-911541-85-3
13-digit 978-0-911541-85-4

Table of Contents

Introduction

Since you are reading this page, I assume You did exactly what I hoped you would do. I put the subtitle "Don't Read This!" under "Introduction" in hopes that you would be curious about why I did not want you to read this. (Actually I did want you to read it.)

I am sure you have seen study guides before. Maybe you've even used a few. I and, I am sure, your instructor want you to use this one extensively. If you do, I think you will find the course will be much easier for you.

The study guide is divided into chapters identical to those used in the *People and Politics* textbook.

Each chapter is divided into headings entitled

Learning Objectives
Didn't you know there were some?

Chapter Outline
Yucky, but useful!

Important Terms
Caution: They may shock you!

Multiple Choice Questions
Yeah!

Fill-in-the-Blank Questions
Boo! Hiss!

True/False Questions
Absolutely Vicious!

Discussion Questions
Totally gross, but ya gotta write!

Using Your Little Grey Cells
Hercule Poirot would be proud!

Before you get spastic trying to find them, I did not put the answers in the study guide. You are supposed to find them yourself. However, your instructor does have a copy of the answers.

May your semester be a great one!
Mary Kate Hiatt, Ph.D
June 19, 2009

CHAPTER 1

Challenges
to American Democracy

Learning Objectives

After reading and studying the chapter on the challenges to American democracy, you should have a better understanding of the following:

1. The "experimental" nature of the United States government;
2. What challenges the United States faces both at home and abroad;
3. The meaning of the term government;
4. The origins of the state and of the government;
5. The purposes of government;
6. The nature of the United States government;
7. The requirements of a democracy;
8. What the future holds for American democracy.

Chapter Outline

I.   The Great Experiment
   A.   Idea of democracy new
   B.   Federation type government unique in 18th century
   C.   Multi-national character of the United States
   D.   Reasons for settlement in English colonies
      • Seeking riches
      • Seeking religious and political freedom
      • Escaping poverty
   E.   Economic and political stability of the United States

II.   The Challenges to American Democracy
   A.   Military challenges
      • Cold War
      • Terrorism
      • Bush Doctrine
   B.   Economic challenges
      • Stagflation
      • Globalization of trade
      • Downsizing
      • European Union
      • NAFTA
      • Growth of American and global economies
      • Major trends
         • Size and growth of the American economy
         • Creation of a permanent two-tier economy
         • Explosion of M3
         • Decline of American tech advantage
         • Rising budget deficit, debt, and decline of U.S. dollar

C. Equality
- Liberty
  - Freedom of action without government interference
- Equality
  - Political
  - Social
  - Opportunity

D. Confidence in government
- Decline of political parties
- Rise of partisanship
- Attitude that government is incompetent

IV. Understanding Government
A. Definition of government
- Legal structure containing formal "rulers" who perform governmental functions
- Functions
  - Initiate and pass laws
  - Execute and administer laws
  - Interpret laws and resolve disputes

B. Origins of the state and of the government
- Evolutionary theory: government just developed over time
- Force theory: the strongest people govern
- Social contract theory
  - John Locke (1689)
  - Government by consent of the people

C. Purposes of government
- To protect people's natural, inalienable rights
- "Establish justice"
- "Promote the general welfare"
- "Secure . . . liberty"
- Interpretation of purposes change with time

V. The American Government
A. Representative democracy: indirect democracy through elected representatives
B. Constitutionalism: places limits on government
C. Separation of powers: governmental functions reside in three different places
D. Federalism: governmental authority divided between central government and state governments
E. Checks and balance system: each branch of government has some power over the others

14th edition

VI. America's Future
    A. Many challenges to the United States
    B. Requirements of a democracy to meet challenges
- Education
- Information
- Involvement

Important Terms

Bill of Rights	Downsizing	Check & Balance System
Equality	Federalism	Communist Manifesto
Taliban	Force theory	Representative Democracy
Democracy	Cold war	Direct democracy
The Euro	Bush Doctrine	Indirect democracy
Al Qaeda	Thomas Jefferson	Evolutionary theory
Karl Marx	Osama bin Laden	Multi-national state
Housing bubble	Terrorism	Budget deficit
NAFTA	OPEC	National debt
European Union	M3	DOT.com bubble
KGB	NATO	Separation of Powers
Stagflation	John Locke	Constitutionalism
Government	State	Social contract theory

Multiple Choice Questions

Circle the number of the correct choice.

1. _____ the military alliance formed after World War II, consisting of the United States and a number of its allies.

    1) NAFTA
    2) NATO
    3) European Union
    4) Allied Powers
    5) Camp David Accords

14th edition

2. Much of what Americans do know about their government regarding the rights of people accused of crimes comes from

   1) newspapers
   2) American government classes
   3) television
   4) talking to other people
   5) their experiences in the criminal courts.

3. A period of time when investment in companies that sold goods and services online spiked significantly is called the Dot.com _____.

   1) Peak
   2) Bust
   3) Summit
   4) Bubble
   5) Balloon.

4. To most Americans the term equality means

   1) everyone should have equal amounts of the world's resources
   2) everyone should be treated the same under the law
   3) everyone should have an equal opportunity to compete for the world's resources
   4) only #2 and #3
   5) all-- #1, #2, and #3.

5. The quantity of output that each worker can produce in one year is called

   1) Gross Domestic Product
   2) Gross National Product
   3) Worker productivity
   4) Worker adaptability
   5) National wealth

6. The theory of the origin of states and governments that claims they just developed over the course of time is referred to as the

   1) Force theory
   2) Evolutionary theory
   3) Revolutionary theory
   4) Social contract theory
   5) Democratic theory.

5
Chapter 1

14th edition

7. The theory of the origin of states and governments that claims they developed because some people were physically more powerful than others and, therefore, could make other people do their bidding is referred to as the

    1) force theory
    2) evolutionary theory
    3) revolutionary theory
    4) social contract theory
    5) democratic theory.

8. John Locke is associated with the theory of the origin of the state called the

    1) force theory
    2) evolutionary theory
    3) revolutionary theory
    4) social contract theory
    5) democratic theory.

9. The Declaration of Independence indicates that the writer believed in a particular theory of the origin of the state called the

    1) force theory
    2) evolutionary theory
    3) revolutionary theory
    4) social contract theory
    5) democratic theory.

10. The theory of the origin of states and governments that claims they developed when people made agreements among themselves to form the state and the government is referred to as the

    1) revolutionary theory
    2) social contract theory
    3) evolutionary theory
    4) democratic theory
    5) force theory.

11. The term *constitutionalism* specifically refers to

    1) a federal form of government
    2) limitations on governments
    3) representative democracy
    4) a presidential form of government
    5) direct democracy.

Chapter 1

14th edition

12. The United States government is characterized by

    1) decentralization
    2) separation of powers
    3) representative government
    4) only #2 and #3
    5) all--#1, #2, and #3.

13. An organized political society that recognizes no higher authority other than its own laws is called a (an)

    1) government
    2) state
    3) nation
    4) confederation
    5) empire

14. An economic period characterized by high inflation and high unemployment is known as

    1) equilibrium
    2) disequilibrium
    3) deflation
    4) inflation
    5) stagflation

15. The ____ is the name of the political organization, made up of Islamic extremists, who ran Afghanistan before the "War on Terrorism" began.

    1) Al Qaeda
    2) Mosad
    3) Taliban
    4) Jihad
    5) Shia

16. An economic alliance of countries that are major oil producers that contributed to the stagflation of the 1970s in the United States was

    1) KGB
    2) OPEC
    3) NATO
    4) EU
    5) UNESCO

14th edition

17. The United States was instrumental in forming NAFTA in response to the economic threat of the _____, another economic alliance, of which the United State is not a member.

    1) North Atlantic Treaty Organization
    2) European Steel and Coal Community
    3) Taipei Group
    4) European Union
    5) Organization of American States

18. A new American foreign policy announced by the George W. Bush Administration stated that the United States would use preemptive strikes against its enemies. The term preemptive in this context means the attacks would be

    1) necessary.
    2) in retaliation for strikes against the United States.
    3) only strong enough to disrupt the enemy.
    4) powerful enough to destroy the enemy.
    5) prior to any attacks on the United States by an enemy.

19. One of the following would be considered a serious threat to the interests of the United States. Which one?

    1) The increasing dollar-amount of imports into the United States
    2) Toyota Corporation's setting up an automobile assembly plant in Idaho
    3) United States exporting home computer technology
    4) Mexico sending thousands of students to study at American universities.
    5) OPEC increasing crude oil output.

Fill-in-the-Blank Questions

Write the appropriate word or words in the blanks provided.

1. The economic confederation made up of the United States, Canada, and Mexico is called _____ .

2. A country with many different races, ethnic groups, and nationalities is called a (an) _____ state.

3. The social contract theory claims that the purpose of government is

    _____ .

14th edition

4. One of the contributing factors to acts of terrorism is the _____ distribution of the world's resources.

5. The American definition of equality implies _____ equality, _____ equality, and equality of _____ .

6. The term _____ is a type of government in which the people elect others to make governmental policy instead of making these decisions directly themselves.

7. In the United States, the division of powers of government between a central government and state governments is called _____ .

8. At the national level, division of the functions of government into three branches is referred to as _____ .

9. A characteristic of the United States government which allows each branch to control or prevent the actions of the other branches and which gives each branch substantially equal amounts of authority is called a system of _____ .

10. A (An) _____ is a legal structure that houses the formal rulers who initiate and pass laws, execute and administer laws, and resolve disputes and interpret laws.

11. The total money supply of a country in economic terms is known as _____ .

12. The amount of money the United States government owes to the citizens, banks, insurance companies, and other countries such as China is known as the _____ .

13. The currency used in the European Union is called the _____ .

14. Actions of non-governmental groups or secret agents of a state who commit violent acts primarily against civilians are defined by the State Department as acts of _____ .

15. The term _____ refers to laying off or firing employees in an effort to reduce costs in order to meet world competition.

16. The term _____ refers to the time in the second half of the twentieth century when the United States and the former Soviet Union were bitter enemies.

9

Chapter 1

17.   The first ten amendments to the United States Constitution are collectively known as the _____.

18.   Born in Saudi Arabia, _____, this man founded the Al Qaeda terrorist network and helped plan the 9/11 attacks on the United States.

19.   The document, the _____written by Marx and Engels, that sets forth some of the principles of a so-called socialist dictatorship of the working class.

20.   The term _____ comes from Greek words meaning "rule by the people."

21.   The authors of "The Communist Manifesto" were Friedrich Engels and _____.

22.   A _____ occurs when governments' annual spending is greater than their annual revenues.

23.   In the former Soviet Union, the secret police was known as the _____.

24.   Al Qaeda arose out of the _____ who ruled Afghanistan for several years until 2001 when they were essentially removed by a United States invading force.

25.   The trade alliance formed among the United States, Canada, and Mexico is called _____.

True/False Questions

Write the correct response in the blank provided.

1. The oldest written constitution still in use in the world today is the United States Constitution. _____

2. The Constitution of the United States has been used in this country since the end of the American Revolution in 1781. _____

3. "From each according to his ability, to each according to his need" is a statement found in the Preamble to the United States Constitution and was taken from the Declaration of Independence. _____

4. Representative democracy is another term used to mean indirect democracy. _____

5. Americans are generally not well informed about their government. _____

6. The President of the United States possesses "emergency" powers with which he/she can disband Congress during an extreme national crisis. _____

7. The Constitution requires that English be the official language of the United States. _____

8. All persons accused of crimes in the United States have the right to a trial by jury. _____

9. The Constitution does not guarantee a free, public education to anyone in the United States. _____

10. Democratic governments were quite common in the 18th century. _____

11. Spain, France, and Portugal viewed their colonies in the Americas primarily as places to use for the benefit of the mother country. _____

12. The United States has been relatively free of some of the radical movements, found frequently in other parts of the world, probably because of political and economic stability. _____

13. World opinion does not usually support retaliation against terrorists for their actions. _____

14. Most governments in the world today operate under some form of a written constitution. _____

15. There is no disagreement among Americans that in the United States everyone really does have an equal opportunity to compete for the world's resources. _____

16. Political parties in the United States have declined in influence over the past half century. _____

17. Americans generally think highly of the ability of the United States government to provide the services they expect. _____

18. The purposes of all governments around the world are the same. _____

19. Both democratic and non-democratic governments perform legislative, executive, and judicial functions. _____

11
Chapter 1

14th edition

20. Countries outside the Middle East rarely get involved in conflicts in the Middle East because that part of the world has nothing of real strategic interest. _____

21. The Obama administration is trying to reduce the budget deficit and the national debt by reducing spending on social programs. _____

22. Americans save very little of their incomes. _____

23. Today, most countries have too large a population even to consider using direct democracy. _____

24. Since the end of the Cold War, external threats to the United States have been minimal. _____

25. Housing bubbles do not occur in the United States because of its stable political and economic environment. _____

26. The United States economic output is rapidly being overtaken by the economies of Japan and China. _____

27. Another name for the *budget deficit* is the *national debt.* _____

28. George Washington was the author of the Declaration of Independence. _____

29. Direct Democracy is a popular form of government around the world because it is not complicated and citizens like it. _____

Discussion Questions

Use your own paper to answer the following questions.

1. Why do many countries react unfavorably to those who advocate retaliation against terrorists?

2. Why is a decline in oil prices both good and bad for the United States economy?

3. Why are foreign imports so numerous in the United States and not so numerous in some other countries?

14th edition

4. Explain the meaning of equality in American political philosophy?

5. If the vast majority of Americans agree that everyone should have equal opportunity to compete for the world's resources, why is there still a problem in achieving this goal?

6. Explain the three theories concerning the origin of the state and of the government. Why do most Americans accept the social contract theory as the correct one?

7. What three things does a democracy require people to do in order for the system to function as it was intended? Do you fulfill these requirements? Explain your answer.

Using Your Little Gray Cells

1. Give a summary of the "Whitewater" scandal surrounding President Bill Clinton. What do you think a president should do when he or she is confronted with such a scandal? Explain.

2. Write a report in which you summarize the events surrounding the Iran/Hostage Crisis. Then compose an argument stating what you would have done had you been President of the United States. Cite reasons for your actions or lack of action. Once you have stated what you would have done and why, try to predict what the results of your actions might have been in regard to the hostages, the reactions of Iran, and the reactions of the rest of the world in general.

3. Write a report detailing the "Watergate" incident of the early 1970s. Include any changes in the law that occurred as a result of this incident. What would you have done if you had been President Nixon and discovered that some of your supporters had broken into the Democratic Party National Headquarters? Explain how your actions would have been "better" than President Nixon's.

4. Get in groups of three or four and select someone to be the group's reporter. "Brain storm" the following scenario. You are the leader of a traditional and very poor African country. You believe that to get your country on the road to prosperity, the country must modernize, but you meet with serious resistance from some other political leaders, some powerful religious leaders, and even most of the population. What are you going to do?

5. Either alone or in groups, assume you are members of an organization called Direct Action that is carrying out terrorist acts against the United States. Identify as many "reasons" that Direct Action would assert for its use of terrorism against the United States. Are any of these reasons valid? Defend your response.

6. *Parade Magazine*, in an article dated February 24, 2002, commented on three myths that had arisen in the American population concerning the Vietnam War. They were as follows:

    Myth #1: American soldiers were very young and not well educated. The fact is the average age was 23, and 79 percent of the troops had at least a high-school education.

    Myth #2: The overwhelming majority of the American soldiers were poor blacks. The real story is that, of the 58,000 American soldiers who died in this war, 30 percent came from the lowest third in income, but 26 percent came from the highest third in income. Only 12.5 percent were black. That figure is approximately the percentage of black people in the U.S. population as a whole.

    Myth #3: Many young men were jailed as draft evaders during the Vietnam War. The fact is that, although a half a million did illegally avoid the draft, only 9000 were ever convicted of this crime.

    Organize into groups of four or five and discuss the possible reasons these myths might have developed. Who would have benefited by propagating these myths and how would they have benefited?

We hold these truths to be self evident;
that all men are created equal,
that they are endowed by their Creator
with certain unalienable rights,
that among these are life, liberty, and
the pursuit of happiness.

Thomas Jefferson, 1776

Chapter 2

The American Experience

Learning Objectives

After reading and studying the chapter on the American experience, you should
have a better understanding of the following:

1. Why the American Revolution was fought;
2. The Articles of Confederation and the problems they created;
3. The reasons why the constitutional convention was called;
4. What is in the Constitution and why;
5. The process of ratification;
6. Differing interpretations of the intent of the Constitution;
7. The future of the Constitution.

Chapter Outline

I. The American Revolution
  A. Why revolution
    1. Political discontent
    2. Not everyone loyal to Britain
    3. Natural course of events
  B. Justification
    1. John Locke: Social Contract Theory
      a. Men born with natural rights
      b. Governments formed by social compact to protect rights
      c. People could revolt if government failed to protect rights
    2. Used by Jefferson in Declaration of Independence
  C. Was American Revolution a real Revolution
    1. Most agree it was a real revolution because
      a. Political philosophy of Americans on power and rights differed from British
      b. Governmental institutions that arose were unique
    2. Others disagree because
      a. Colonists merely regaining rights they were supposed to have
      b. Merely a revolt of mercantile class (merchants)
      c. Very little changed in America after Revolution

II. Building a Nation
  A. Articles of Confederation
    1. First constitution, 1781-1789
    2. Structure

16

Chapter 2

a. Loose union of states
b. One-house Congress
c. Each state had one vote
d. No judicial branch
e. No executive branch
f. States remained independent except in
    (1) Foreign policy
    (2) Matters necessary for common good of all states
    (3) National security

B. Problems
1. No direct taxes (taxes on people)
2. Military dependent on volunteers from states
3. No regulation of interstate commerce
4. No executive or judicial branches to enforce or interpret laws

III. Call for Change
A. Conditions in country amounted to political and economic disaster
B. Constitutional convention called in Annapolis, Maryland
1. 1786
2. Unsuccessful because of lack of attendance
C. Another convention called in Philadelphia, Pennsylvania
1. 1787
2. All states except Rhode Island attended

IV. Philadelphia Convention
A. May, 1787
B. Disagreement over need for convention
1. Some argued that country's problems merely result of poor, worldwide, economic conditions
2. Shays's Rebellion changed most minds
C. Pre-convention issues
1. Need to establish legitimacy
2. Need for secrecy
3. Purpose of convention
a. Merely revise Articles of Confederation or
b. Write new constitution
D. The convention at work
1. Agreements at the outset
a. Federalism: division of powers of government between national government and state governments
b. Separation of powers: division of national government's powers into three separate branches-- legislative, executive, judicial

17

Chapter 2

      c. Property protection: not protected enough under Articles of Confederation
- 2. Virginia Plan
    - a. Largely work of James Madison
    - b. Supported by large states (large populations)
    - c. Introduced by Edmund Randolph
    - d. Included
        - (1) Bicameral legislature with representation based on population of each state
        - (2) National executive
        - (3) National judiciary
- 3. New Jersey Plan
    - a. Introduced by William Paterson (name spelled with one "t")
    - b. Supported by small states (small populations)
    - c. Included
        - (1) Unicameral Congress with equal representation for all states (one vote each)
        - (2) Congressional powers
            - (a) Tax
            - (b) Regulate trade
            - (c) Force states to obey national laws
        - (3) Multiple executive
        - (4) Supreme court
- 4. Great Compromise
    - a. Resolved disagreement between large and small states over representation in Congress
    - b. Proposed
        - (1) Bicameral legislature
        - (2) Representation in lower house based on population of each state
        - (3) Representation in upper house based on each state's having two representatives

- 5. Other compromises
    - a. 3/5 of slaves counted for population and taxation purposes
    - b. Importation of slaves was to end in 1808
    - c. No export taxes
    - d. Exclusive national-government regulation of interstate and foreign commerce

V. Ratification
  A. Nine states required for approval
  B. Ratification by special convention in each state

Chapter 2

C. Two opposing groups developed
   1. Federalists supported ratification
   2. Anti-Federalists opposed ratification
D. Struggle for ratification produced
   1. *The Federalist*
      a. Series of newspaper articles in New York written to urge support for ratification of new constitution
      b. Still serves today as excellent explanation of Constitution
   2. Bill of Rights
      a. Resulted from Anti-Federalists' objection that central government might become abusive if rights not spelled out in Constitution
      b. Federalists agreed to support amending Constitution, once it was ratified, to include Bill of Rights because they needed support from Anti-Federalists for ratification in New York and Virginia

VI. A Different Interpretation of the Constitution
   A. Charles Beard's *An Economic Interpretation of the Constitution* (1913)
      1. Convention delegates motivated by economic self-interest
      2. Most were propertied class who suffered economic loss under Articles of Confederation
      3. Therefore, Constitution favored interests of propertied class
   B. Forrest McDonald's *We the People* (1958)
      1. Economic self-interest too simplistic as explanation of Constitution
      2. Convention delegates' motivations for writing Constitution mixed
      3. Constitution represents interests of many classes of people
VII. Constitutional Concepts
   A. Constitutionalism
      1. Written constitution
      2. Limits government
   B. Separation of powers
      1. Functions of government separated
      2. Three branches of government
         a. Legislative--makes laws
         b. Executive--enforces laws
         c. Judicial--interprets laws
   C. Checks and balance
      1. Each branch of government has essentially equal amount of power and has some control over others

19

Chapter 2

14th Edition

2. Examples
   a. Veto power of president
   b. Judicial-review power of courts
   c. Electoral college system
3. Judicial review
   a. Power of courts to determine constitutionality of laws and executive actions
   b. First time used in court case *Marbury v. Madison* (1803)

VIII. Surviving the Test of Time
   A. United States Constitution oldest constitution still in use
   B. Reasons for longevity
      1. Interpretation
         a. Constitution interpreted to fit times
         b. Constitution quite brief
         c. Constitution not detailed--broad outline of government
      2. Custom and usage
         a. Institutions and procedures not mentioned in Constitution
            just developed over time to fit current needs
         b. Examples
            (1) Political parties
            (2) Electors associated with parties rather than independent
      3. Amendments
         a. Formal amendments change Constitution when necessary
         b. Twenty-seven added thus far
         c. Proposal of amendments
            (1) By 2/3 vote of <u>both</u> houses of Congress
            (2) By special convention called at request of 2/3 of states' legislatures
            (3) All amendments thus far proposed by 2/3 vote of both houses of Congress
         d. Ratification of amendments
            (1) By 3/4 of states' legislatures
            (2) By special conventions in 3/4 of states
            (3) Congress chooses which method of ratification will be used for each amendment
            (4) All amendments except 21st Amendment ratified by 3/4 of state legislatures

IX. Looking Back--Looking Ahead
   A. Framers saw a need for compromise

20

Chapter 2

14th Edition

B. Therefore, no one completely satisfied with Constitution
C. Compromise still necessary in today's society
D. Constitution likely to continue serving needs of United States in years to come because of its flexibility

Important Terms

1781	Separation of Powers	Great Compromise
1787	Constitutionalism	Interstate Commerce
1789	Federalism	Bicameral Legislature
Articles of Confederation	Formal Amendment	Shays's Rebellion
Judicial Review	New Jersey Plan	Direct Taxes
Social Contract Theory	Virginia Plan	John Locke
Thomas Jefferson	Check & Balance System	Unicameral Legislature

Multiple Choice Questions

Circle the number of the correct answer.

1. A government which has limits placed upon it in a written constitution is said to be *specifically* characterized by

    (1) separation of powers
    (2) constitutionalism
    (3) federalism
    (4) *laissez faire* capitalism
    (5) authoritarianism.

2. When a government's functions are divided into three parts at the national level (a legislative, an executive, and a judicial branch), it is said to be characterized by

    (1) separation of powers
    (2) constitutionalism
    (3) federalism
    (4) capitalism
    (5) authoritarianism.

3. The president's veto power is an example of

    (1) authoritarianism
    (2) separation of powers
    (3) constitutionalism
    (4) the checks and balance system
    (5) democracy.

4. When each branch of government is dependent on the other branches or is limited in some way by them, the government is said to be operating under a system of

    (1) democracy
    (2) separation of powers
    (3) constitutionalism
    (4) checks and balance
    (5) authoritarianism.

5. The power of a court to declare acts of Congress, acts of state legislatures, or actions of presidents unconstitutional is called

    (1) judicial review
    (2) separation of powers
    (3) authoritarianism
    (4) democracy
    (5) republicanism.

6. Theory that states that governments were formed by agreements, or compacts, among men was written about by the English philosopher

    (1) Elbridge Gerry
    (2) John Locke
    (3) Roger Sherman
    (4) Thomas Jefferson
    (5) Richard Henry Lee.

7. The author of the Declaration of Independence was

    (1) Elbridge Gerry
    (2) John Locke
    (3) Roger Sherman
    (4) Thomas Jefferson
    (5) Richard Henry Lee.

8. The first constitution used in the United States was the

    (1) Declaration of Independence
    (2) Constitution of 1789
    (3) By-laws of the Continental Congress
    (4) Articles of Confederation
    (5) Declaration of the Rights of Man.

9. The Articles of Confederation were proposed by

    (1) Richard Henry Lee
    (2) Thomas Jefferson
    (3) Alexander Hamilton
    (4) James Madison
    (5) William Paterson.

10. The Articles of Confederation went into effect in the year

    (1) 1776
    (2) 1781
    (3) 1783
    (4) 1787
    (5) 1789.

11. Under the Articles of Confederation there was

    (1) no executive branch
    (2) no judicial branch
    (3) a unicameral congress
    (4) both #1 and #2
    (5) all--#1, #2, and #3.

12. The New Jersey Plan

    (1) was radically different from the Articles of Confederation
    (2) was favored by states with large populations
    (3) was favored by states with small populations
    (4) proposed a bicameral congress
    (5) proposed a supreme court appointed by the legislative branch.

13. A major problem for the central government under the Articles of Confederation was that it could not

    (1) declare war without the consent of the states
    (2) negotiate treaties
    (3) levy direct taxes on the people
    (4) borrow money
    (5) settle boundary disputes between states if one arose.

14. The Constitution of the United States, written in Philadelphia, <u>went into effect</u> in the year

    (1) 1776
    (2) 1781
    (3) 1783
    (4) 1787
    (5) 1789.

15. The Articles of Confederation did not allow the national government the power to

    (1) impose direct taxes
    (2) impose indirect taxes
    (3) establish a legislative branch
    (4) send ambassadors to foreign countries
    (5) receive ambassadors from foreign countries.

16. The ideas in the Virginia Plan were primarily those of

    (1) Edmund Randolph
    (2) James Madison
    (3) Roger Sherman
    (4) William Paterson
    (5) Elbridge Gerry.

17. Disputes arose at the Philadelphia convention concerning

    (1) slavery
    (2) representation in Congress
    (3) separation of powers
    (4) both #1 and #2
    (5) All--#1, #2, and #3.

18. The Constitution of the United States was <u>written</u> in the year

   (1) 1776
   (2) 1781
   (3) 1783
   (4) 1787
   (5) 1789.

19. The controversy over how to count slaves for purposes of representation in Congress and taxation was resolved when it was decided that

   (1) all slaves should be counted
   (2) two-thirds of the slaves should be counted
   (3) three-fourths of the slaves should be counted
   (4) one-half of the slaves should be counted
   (5) three-fifths of the slaves should be counted.

20. To ratify the new constitution the

   (1) approval of all states was needed
   (2) approval of six states was needed
   (3) approval of seven states was needed
   (4) approval of nine states was needed
   (5) approval of eleven states was needed.

21. One of the following is not mentioned in the Constitution but has come into usage by custom:

   (1) political parties
   (2) the checks and balance system
   (3) federalism
   (4) laws against treason
   (5) both #1 and #4.

22. An amendment may be <u>proposed</u> by

   (1) a two-thirds vote of <u>both</u> houses of Congress
   (2) a two-thirds vote of the Congress <u>as a whole</u>
   (3) a special convention called at the request of two-thirds of the state legislatures
   (4) both #1 and #3
   (5) both #2 and #3.

23. An amendment may be ratified by

   (1) three-fourths of the state legislatures
   (2) special conventions in three-fourths of the states
   (3) a three-fourths vote of <u>both</u> houses of Congress
   (4) both #1 and #2
   (5) both #1 and #3.

Fill-in-the-Blank Questions

Write the appropriate word or words in the blanks provided.

1. A series of newspaper articles printed in New York urging ratification of the new constitution is known as _____ .

2. Those who supported ratification of the new Constitution were called _____ .

3. Those who opposed ratification of the new Constitution were called _____ .

4. The delegates to the Philadelphia convention agreed that the new government should be a (an) _____ form of government in which the people would rule through elected representatives.

5. The _____ Compromise settled the dispute between the large states and the small states over representation in the legislative branch.

6. The event that changed most delegates' thinking about the need for a constitutional convention was _____ .

7. The first time the Supreme Court used its power of judicial review was in the case _____ in 1803.

8. *The Federalist* was written by _____, _____, and _____ .

9. A legislative body made up of only one chamber ("house") is known as a _____ legislature.

10. Coker Fudlinker lives in Hot Coffee, Mississippi. He visited his brother Bentley in Bunky, Louisiana, where Coker bought a new Ford. When the visit was over, Coker returned to Hot Coffee with his new car. By buying a car in one state and returning to his home state with it, Coker has engaged in a type of trade known as _____, which is regulated by the national government.

True/False Questions

Write the correct response in the blanks provided.

1. The Constitution does not require that states follow the same principle of separation of powers that the national government does. _____

2. Under the Articles of Confederation, each state had two votes in the Congress, just as they do in the Senate today. _____

3. Under the Articles of Confederation, each state retained its sovereignty except in areas specifically stated in the Articles. _____

4. Raising and maintaining an army and a navy was not a problem for the central government under the Articles of Confederation. _____

5. Under the Articles of Confederation, states were forbidden to impose discriminatory regulations or taxes on goods from other states. _____

6. The first president of the United States under the Articles of Confederation was George Washington. _____

7. At the outset of the Philadelphia convention, everyone was in agreement that a national convention was necessary. _____

8. The Philadelphia convention was actually called merely to amend the Articles of Confederation, rather than to write a new constitution. _____

9. As soon as the ninth state had ratified, the new constitution went into effect. _____

10. When the new constitution was finally finished, almost all the delegates were pleased with what they had written. _____

11. Under the Articles of Confederation, the owners of large businesses, financiers, and merchants had done well economically; therefore, they saw no need for radical changes in the government. _____

27

Chapter 2

12. The Constitution is a very long, specific, and detailed document so that future generations will have no difficulty deciding what the government is supposed to do. _____

13. The American government was the first to use the concept of a written constitution. _____

14. All amendments to the Constitution have been ratified by state legislatures. _____

Discussion Questions

Use your own paper to answer the following questions.

1. Why did American colonists believe it necessary to revolt against British rule?

2. How did John Locke's theories serve as a justification for the American Revolution?

3. What arguments are offered in favor of the claim that the American Revolution was not a real revolution?

4. How did Shays's Rebellion relate to the writing of a new constitution?

5. Why did the delegates to the Philadelphia convention agree to a rule of secrecy? Do you think the convention should have been "open?" Explain.

6. Why did Rhode Island boycott the Philadelphia convention?

7. How were the Virginia Plan and the New Jersey Plan similar and how were they different?

8. Why did the southern states want the national government to be denied the power to levy export taxes?

9. What was Charles Beard's main point in his work *An Economic Interpretation of the Constitution*? Do you agree or disagree with it? Explain.

10. What arguments does Forrest McDonald advance in *We the People* to counter Beard's viewpoint?

Using Your Little Gray Cells

1. Using the copy of the Declaration of Independence, write a brief report on which concepts you would agree or disagree with in the context of today's American society? Explain your reasoning.

2. The concept of democracy was discussed throughout the constitutional convention of 1787. Go to your school's library and find the *Diaries of the Federal Constitutional Convention* by Max Farrand, which gives an account of the proceedings of the Philadelphia convention. Write a report describing what the convention delegates thought about democracy. Based on what you have discovered, conclude your paper with an explanation of whether people today would agree that the convention delegates were really democratic in their thinking compared to what people believe "democratic" means today.

3. Find a copy of the Canadian Constitution. (If one is not available in the library, write the Canadian embassy in Washington, D.C., or one can be found on the Internet by using a such engine such as Yahoo or Google.) Compare the structure of the government of Canada as <u>described</u> in its constitution to the structure of the United States government as <u>described</u> in the American Constitution showing the differences and similarities.

4. The Declaration of Independence, written by Thomas Jefferson in 1776, stated that people had the inalienable right to "the pursuit of happiness." However, he did not define the term *happiness*.. The ancient Greek philosopher Socrates (circa 469 BC to 399 BC), asked the great thinkers of his day to define the concept pleasure, or happiness. They replied by saying that pleasure, or happiness, was the absence of pain. Socrates was not satisfied with that definition. In groups, discuss what you think Jefferson meant by "pursuit of happiness" in 1776 and then what you think it means to Americans today. Be prepared to discuss your ideas with the rest of the class.

Chapter 3

The Federal System:
A Blessing or a Curse?

Learning Objectives

After reading and studying the chapter on federalism, you should have a better understanding of the following:

1. The meaning of the terms *unitary government, federalism,* and *confederation*;
2. The shortcomings of federalism;
3. Why the United States has a federal system;
4. The structure of American federalism.

Chapter Outline

I. Defining Federalism
   A. Governmental choices at the Philadelphia convention
      1. Unitary government
         a. One central government
         b. May create regional governments
            (1) These only carry out policy made by central government
            (2) They do not make policy
            (3) May be abolished by central government any time
         c. Most popular form of government in democracies today
         d. Examples
            (1) Great Britain
            (2) France
      2. Federal government
         a. One central government and several regional governments (e.g., states in the United States)
         b. Each government assigned substantial authority independent of others
         c. Examples
            (1) United States
            (2) Canada
            (3) Mexico
      3. Confederation government
         a. One central government and several regional governments
         b. Regional governments essentially sovereign
         c. Regional governments not subject to much control by central government
         d. First United States government a confederation
         e. Current example: the United Nations

14th edition

II.   Federalism's Shortcomings
      A. Extremely complicated
      B. Can hinder solving of national problems
      C. Creates differences in treatment of people in different states
         1. Punishment for crimes
         2. Education
         3. Social welfare benefits
      D. Creates problems by multiple taxation
      E. Promotes unhealthy competition among states for businesses and industries
      F. Creates administrative inefficiency
         1. Some states too small or too large
         2. Boundaries essentially cannot be changed

III. Why Federalism for the United States?
      A. Fear of unrestrained, powerful, central governments
      B. Intense loyalty to states
      C. Confederation did not work

IV.   Structure of American Federalism
      A. Powers of national government
         1. All powers of national government delegated by people through Constitution
         2. Three types of delegated powers
            a. Enumerated (or expressed) powers
               (1) Specifically listed in Constitution
               (2) Establish post offices
               (3) Regulate interstate and foreign commerce
               (4) Tax
            b. Implied powers
               (1) Powers that can be reasonably inferred (implied) from expressed powers
               (2) Come from "Elastic Clause" of Constitution
               (3) Establishing the Air Force
               (4) Defining and punishing crimes such as bank robbery
            c. Inherent powers
               (1) Supreme Court defined these in *United States v. Curtiss-Wright Export Corporation*
               (2) Powers that national government can exercise merely because it is a national government
               (3) Explore space
               (4) Acquire territory
               (5) Regulate immigration
      B. Powers of state government
         1. All state powers reserved (Tenth Amendment)

32
Chapter 3

14th edition

2. Powers not granted to national government by Constitution, nor denied to states, reserved to states or to people
3. Most governmental activities within reserved powers of state
4. Examples
   a. Education
   b. Traffic laws
   c. Police and fire protection
   d. Aid to homeless
   e. Unemployment compensation
C. Powers shared by states and national government
   1. Called concurrent powers
   2. Examples
      a. Tax and spend
      b. Borrow money
      c. Take private property for public use
      d. Establish courts
D. Limitations and obligations of national government
   1. Limitations (Article I, Section 9)
      a. No bills of attainder: legislative acts that provide for punishment of individual without benefit of trial
      b. No *ex post facto* laws: retroactive criminal laws
      c. No suspension of writ of *habeas corpus* except under specific conditions
      d. Other specific limitations listed in Bill of Rights
   2. Obligations (Article IV)
      a. Guarantee republican form of government in all states
         (1) Term *republican* not clearly defined in Constitution
         (2) Constitution not clear about which branch of national government is supposed to enforce this provision
      b. Protect each state against invasion and domestic violence (i.e., rebellion)
         (1) Invasion only occurred once during War of 1812
         (2) National troops used 16 times to put down domestic violence
            (a) Can be done without state's consent
            (b) Little Rock, Arkansas (1957)
            (c) Oxford, Mississippi (1962)
            (d) Tuscaloosa, Alabama (1963)
            (e) Detroit, Michigan (1968)
            (f) Los Angeles, California (1992)
      c. Insure and preserve territory of each state

          (1)   No state can lose territory (without its permission) to form new state

          (2)   No states can be combined (without their permission)

      d.   Insure equal representation of each state in Senate

          (1)   Article V of Constitution

          (2)   Two Senators for each state regardless of size

E. Limitations and obligations of states to national government

   1. Limitations

      a.   Cannot secede from Union

      b.   Cannot coin money

      c.   Cannot make agreements with foreign governments without congressional consent

      d.   Cannot infringe on civil rights of citizens

   2. Obligations

      a.   Hold elections for national offices

      b.   Fill congressional vacancies

      c.   Select presidential electors

      d.   Consider proposed amendments to Constitution

      e.   Recognize Constitution, national laws, and treaties as superior to state laws

      f.   Local governments merely creatures of states; therefore, all obligations and limitations binding upon them also

F. Horizontal federalism: state to state obligations

   1. States' obligations to one another outgrowth of difficulties under Articles of Confederation

   2. Each state must recognize as valid all civil decisions, official records, and judicial judgments of every other state (Full Faith and Credit Clause of Constitution)

   3. Each state must grant same privileges and immunities to nonresidents as it does to its residents

      a.   Found in Privileges and Immunities Clause of Constitution

      b.   Examples

          (1) Use of its courts

          (2) Engage in legitimate businesses

          (3) No extra taxes or restrictions

      c.   Confusion between "rights" and "privileges

          (1) Out-of-state tuition for schools

          (2) Higher fees for out-of-state residents for hunting and fishing licenses

          (3) Out-of-state residents cannot vote or serve on juries

      d.   Supreme Court's attempt to define *residency*

          (1) One year for attending public colleges without extra fees

          (2) Six months for some political privileges

          (3) One day for emergency welfare payments

4. Extradition
    a. Technically known as Interstate Rendition
    b. Return of fugitive to state wherein he/she accused of crime
    b. For all practical purposes now, obligation is mandatory
    c. Usually routine.
    d. Congress authorized governor as agent of extradition
    e. Congress also made fleeing across state lines to avoid prosecution federal crime
5. Interstate compacts
    a. Agreements between or among states to do something jointly
    b. Solve problems between or among states without having to resort to court action
    c. Usually require approval of Congress
    d. Considered legally enforceable contracts

Important Terms

Unitary government
Durational residency
Constitutional government
Enumerated powers
Privileges and immunities
Concurrent powers
Writ of *habeas corpus*
United States v. Curtiss-Wright Export Corporation

Federalism
Extradition
Confederation
Implied powers
Reserved powers
Bill of attainder
Full faith and credit
Interstate Rendition

"Elastic clause"
Interstate compacts
Delegated powers
Ex post facto law
Progressive tax
Regressive tax
Inherent powers

Multiple Choice Questions

Circle the number of the correct answer.

1. A system of government in which there is one central government that actually controls all governmental functions is called a

    (1) confederation
    (2) unitary government
    (3) federation
    (4) dictatorship
    (5) communist government.

2. A system of government in which there is a central government and several regional governments, all of which exercise some powers independent of each other is called a

    (1) confederation
    (2) unitary government
    (3) federation
    (4) dictatorship
    (5) communist government.

3. A system of government in which there is a central government and several regional governments but in which the regional governments are supreme over the central government in most matters is called a

    (1) confederation
    (2) unitary government
    (3) federation
    (4) dictatorship
    (5) communist government.

4. One of the following countries has a unitary government:

    (1) the United States
    (2) Mexico
    (3) Canada
    (4) Switzerland
    (5) Great Britain.

5. One of the following has a federation type government:

    (1) France
    (2) the United States
    (3) Great Britain
    (4) Mexico
    (5) both #2 and # 4.

6. For most of its revenue, the national government of the United States relies primarily on

    (1) indirect taxes
    (2) income taxes
    (3) sales taxes
    (4) excise taxes
    (5) real estate taxes.

14th edition

7. For most of its revenue, the state government relies primarily on

   (1) income taxes
   (2) sales taxes
   (3) indirect taxes
   (4) excise taxes
   (5) real estate taxes.

8. For most of its revenue, the local government relies primarily on

   (1) real estate taxes
   (2) excise taxes
   (3) sales taxes
   (4) indirect taxes
   (5) income taxes.

9. Sales taxes and real estate taxes are examples of

   (1) progressive taxes
   (2) regressive taxes
   (3) excise taxes
   (4) both #1 and #3
   (5) both #2 and #3.

10. Powers of the national government that are specifically listed in the Constitution are called

    (1) enumerated powers
    (2) implied powers
    (3) inherent powers
    (4) concurrent powers
    (5) exclusive powers.

11. Powers of the national government that belong to it merely because it is a national government are called

    (1) enumerated powers
    (2) implied powers
    (3) inherent powers
    (4) concurrent powers
    (5) exclusive powers.

12. Powers of the national government that can be reasonably inferred from those actually stated in the Constitution are called

   (1) enumerated powers
   (2) implied powers
   (3) inherent powers
   (4) concurrent powers
   (5) exclusive powers.

13. One of the following is an inherent power of the national government:

   (1) the power to tax
   (2) the power to acquire territory
   (3) the power to regulate interstate commerce
   (4) the power to establish a post office
   (5) the power to borrow money.

14. One of the following is not a reserved power of the state:

   (1) the power to acquire territory
   (2) the power to provide police protection
   (3) the power to provide education
   (4) the power to provide aid to the homeless
   (5) the power to regulate traffic.

15. One of the following is not a concurrent power:

   (1) the power to borrow money
   (2) the power to tax
   (3) the power to regulate interstate commerce
   (4) the power to take private property for public use
   (5) the power to establish courts.

16. Powers that are shared by both the state and the national governments are called

   (1) enumerated powers
   (2) implied powers
   (3) inherent powers
   (4) concurrent powers
   (5) exclusive powers.

14th edition

17. Legislative acts that inflict punishment on individuals without benefit of a trial are called

    (1) bills of attainder
    (2) *ex post facto* laws
    (3) writs of *habeas corpus*
    (4) double jeopardy
    (5) categorical laws.

18. Laws that increase the penalty for a crime an individual has committed are called

    (1) bills of attainder
    (2) *ex post facto* laws
    (3) writs of *habeas corpus*
    (4) double jeopardy
    (5) categorical laws.

19. Court orders that demand that a person be brought before the court so that he/she may be officially informed of charges against him/her are called

    (1) bills of attainder
    (2) *ex post facto* laws
    (3) *writs of habeas* corpus
    (4) double jeopardy
    (5) categorical laws.

20. Esmerelda Tweedy owns a loan company and lends money to Elmer Turnipseed at a 33% interest rate on June 20, 2010 (the maximum allowable rate on June 20, 2010). On June 21, 2010, the state legislature changes the maximum allowable rate of interest to 25% with a prison term of 5 years for people who lend or had lent money at more than the 25% rate. Such a law would be called a (an)

    (1) bill of attainder
    (2) *ex post facto* law
    (3) *writ of habeas* corpus
    (4) double jeopardy
    (5) categorical law.

14th edition

21. The only time the United States (mainland) was invaded was during the

    (1) War of 1812
    (2) Mexican War
    (3) Spanish/American War
    (4) World War II
    (5) The Cuban Missile Crisis.

22. States are not permitted to

    (1) regulate commerce within their own state
    (2) regulate banks
    (3) coin money
    (4) make treaties with foreign governments
    (5) both #3 and #4.

23. In the United States, the state governments are (Think!)

    (1) confederation governments
    (2) federation governments
    (3) unitary governments
    (4) republican governments
    (5) both #3 and #4.

24. When a state recognizes the validity of a birth certificate issued by another state, the state is said to be

    (1) exercising extradition
    (2) granting full faith and credit
    (3) recognizing an interstate compact
    (4) granting privileges and immunities
    (5) extending the right of a writ of *habeas corpus*.

25. One of the following is <u>not</u> considered among the privileges and immunities that states must extend to the citizens of all states:

    (1) using the state's courts
    (2) operating a hardware store
    (3) attending public schools
    (4) voting
    (5) both #3 and #4.

14th edition

26. Regarding residency, the Supreme Court has ruled that for purposes of receiving emergency welfare benefits a person need only live in a state for a period of

    (1) one day
    (2) one month
    (3) six months
    (4) one year
    (5) eighteen months.

27. Regarding residency, the Supreme Court has ruled that for purposes of attending public colleges without having to pay out-of-state tuition a person need only live in a state for a period of

    (1) one day
    (2) one month
    (3) six months
    (4) one year
    (5) eighteen months.

Fill-in-the-Blank Questions

Write the appropriate word or words in the blanks provided.

1. The term _____ residency means how long a person must live in a state before he/she is considered a legal resident for purposes of voting, receiving welfare benefits, attending public schools, etc.

2. Agreements, known as _____, allow states to work out problems between themselves without resorting to court action.

3. What are the three things that the national government must guarantee to the states?

    (1) _____
    (2) _____
    (3) _____

4. A tax that shifts the burden to those most capable of paying is called a (an) _____ tax.

True/False Questions

Write the correct response in the blanks provided.

1. The Constitution of the United States does not clearly define the meaning of the term *republican* form of government. _____

2. According to constitutional interpretations, the president may send troops to put down domestic violence unless the governor of the state objects. _____

3. Because Alaska, Delaware, North Dakota, South Dakota, Vermont, and Wyoming have very small populations, they are only allowed one senator in the United States Senate. _____

4. Since the Civil War (War Between the States), states are allowed to secede from the Union if they get permission from 2/3 of the other states. _____

5. According to the way the federal system works in the United States, the national government has complete authority over the states if they disagree about some issue. _____

6. When a national law comes in conflict with a state law, the state law takes precedence. _____

7. The federal system of the United States, *according to the Constitution,* sets up a national government, state governments, and local governments, such as counties and cities. _____

8. Most tax revenues go to the national government. _____

9. Large corporations pay about 90% of all federal income taxes. _____

10. For all practical purposes, interstate rendition is required when requested. _____

Discussion Questions

Use your own paper to answer the following questions.

1. What problems result in the field of public education because of federalism?

2. Define a unitary government and a federal government. What argument can be made that the United States should have a unitary government? What argument can be made that the United States should retain its federal form of government? Which do you think the United States should have and why?

Using Your Little Gray Cells

1. There have been a number of Supreme Court cases dealing with the issue of federalism in addition to *McCulloch v. Maryland.* One such case was *National League of Cities v. Usery,* 426 U.S. 833 (1976). Write a report summarizing the facts in the case and the decision of the Court.

2. In the library reference section, find the *Book of the States.* Among other things, it contains comparisons on states' expenditures, revenues, tax sources, program areas, salaries, etc. Compare your state to another state in your region of the country and to another state in another region of the country on one or more of the above categories. How does your state "stack up?"

3. Unitary governments still remain the most used form of government throughout the world. Why do you suppose this is so? Explain.

4. Certain things are not mentioned in the Constitution nor denied to the states that we now know are called reserved powers of the states. Marriage and divorce laws are among those considered reserved to the states. What are your thoughts about this situation: Vermont allows homosexual marriages; Texas does not. Regardless of your opinion of "gay" marriage is, do you think it is fair for homosexuals who want to marry not to be able to do so in Texas when they could if they were in Vermont? At one point in United States history, interracial marriage was forbidden in many states? Regardless of your opinion of interracial marriage is, was it fair, that an interracial couple had to go to another state to marry?

14th edition

Our Federal Union! It must be preserved!

**Toast given at Thomas Jefferson's birthday
celebration, 1830**

*Among the popular and representative systems of
government I do not approve of the federal system:
it is too perfect; and it requires virtues and
talents political much superior to our own.*

**Simone Bolivar, Address to the Congress of
Angostura, 1819**

CHAPTER 4

American Federalism:
Putting the Ideals into Practice

Learning Objectives

After reading and studying the chapter on federalism, you should have a better understanding of the following:

1. The evolution of American federalism;
2. The meaning and complexities of fiscal federalism;
3. What the future holds for American federalism.

Chapter Outline

I. Evolution of American Federalism
   A. Can be viewed in two broad classifications throughout history
      1. Competitive federalism
         a. Rise of the nationalist: *McCulloch v. Maryland*
            (1) Creation of national bank by national government
            (2) Objected to by Democratic-Republican Party
               (a) Not within scope of delegated powers of central government
               (b) Usurped rights of states
            (3) Maryland taxed national bank heavily
            (4) McCulloch, bank cashier, refused to pay tax
            (5) Supreme Court asked to decide
               (a) If national government had power to establish bank
               (b) If state could tax such an agency
            (6) Court ruled in Chief Justice John Marshall's opinion
               (a) National government had implied power to establish bank based on "Necessary and Proper Clause" (Article I, Section 8)
               (b) States cannot tax agency of national government
         b. State-dominated federalism
            (1) Some cooperation between state and national governments before Civil War
            (2) Initially after War, national government maintained advantage over states
            (3) Later, court decisions favored states
               (a) Court turned to Tenth Amendment and carved out state powers untouchable by national government

          (b) Court used Fourteenth Amendment
               declaring corporations legal persons, thus,
               limiting national power to regulate interstate
               commerce
          (c) Period described by Corwin as "dual
               federalism"
             -- National and state governments equal
             -- National government limited to powers
                expressly delegated in Constitution
          (d) *Hammer v. Dagenhart*
             --Challenged constitutionality of Child Labor
                Act of 1916
             --Court ruled national government could not
                prohibit shipment of goods manufactured by
                children who worked more than eight hours per day
                as law provided

   2. Re-emergence of nationalists
      a. Great Depression created need for "new" interpretation
      b. Ultimately Court returned to "loose constructionist," nationalist
          interpretation definitively in *United States v. Darby*
        (1) Minimized importance of Tenth Amendment
        (2) Generally "killed" state-dominated federalism
   3. Cooperative federalism
      a. Few fights today about dominance of national government
      b. States resist attempts of national government to "pull
          back"
        (1) Governing more complex today
        (2) National government money needed in states
B. Twenty-first century problems
   1. Complexity of global interdependency
      a. "New" world we live in demands national attention
      b. Such national attention often cuts into traditional state powers,
          e.g. education
   2. Problems overlapping state boundaries
      a. Pollution
      b. Drug enforcement
      c. Crime control and prevention
      d. Transportation and communication
      e. Energy conservation
      f. Inflation
      g. Resource management
      h. Consumer protection
   3. Inability/refusal of states to meet citizen needs
      a. Some states very poor

14th edition

          b. State where one lives creates inequalities
            (1) Not enough resources to provide educational and other opportunities equal to those in other states
            (2) Racial and other prejudices built into law in some states
    4. Refusal/inability of states to meet underclass demands
    5. Centralization of economic and political power by big business and labor unions
        a. Some states financially unable to fight power of business and labor alone
        b. Turned to national government for help
    6. Interest group activity at national level for favorable treatment
        a. Favorable taxes
        b. Tariffs (import taxes) to protect domestic industries and workers
        c. Subsidies ("welfare" for businesses and farmers)
        d. Causes creation of huge national bureaucracy which creates more national government expansion
    7. National fiscal superiority
        a. National government collects lion's share of taxes
        b. State and local governments expected to provide most costly domestic services
        c. States seek national government's help to provide these services
  C. "Marble-cake" federalism
    1. Used by Morton Grodzins in 1960 to describe today's federalism
    2. Intermingling and intertwining of national, state, and local powers

II. Fiscal Federalism
  A. Defined as states providing services while national government provides much of the money
  B. Unwanted effects
    1. Restricts states' freedom to decide how to provide services and to whom
    2. Federal funds used as weapon to force state/local governments to do things they do not necessarily want to do

III. Assessing Federalism's Advantage
  A. Well suited for large countries
  B. Allows experimentation for new policies without risking entire system
  C. Provides safeguard to freedom
  D. Encourages citizen participation

IV. Recent Developments

14th edition

A. Court sided with states' rights position
B. Constitutional challenges based on
    1. Interstate Commerce Clause
    2. Sovereign Immunity Doctrine
    3. Money issue
C. The Future of Federalism
    1. Unitary view
    2. Self-centered view
    3. Civil libertarian view
    4. Global view

Important Terms

Cross-over sanctions	Sovereign immunity
"Marble-cake" federalism	"Necessary and proper" clause
Tax elasticity	"Dual federalism"
Hammer v. Dagenhart	Strict construction of the
Constitution	Child Labor Act (1916)
Competitive federalism	John Marshall
McCulloch v. Maryland	Fiscal federalism
Cooperative federalism	Mandates
Global view of federalism	*United States v. Darby*
Self-centered view of federalism	*Chisolm v. Georgia*
Civil libertarian view of federalism	Unitary view of federalism
Formula grants	Project grants
Categorical grants	Block grants

Multiple Choice Questions

Circle the number of the correct answer.

1. The relationship between the states and the national government today, which is characterized by the states' delivering services and the national government's paying for those services, is called

    (1) "three-layer-cake" federalism
    (2) "marble-cake" federalism
    (3) fiscal federalism
    (4) state-dominated federalism
    (5) national-government-dominated federalism.

2. The practice of the national government in which it threatens to withhold funds from a project unless the state complies with some demand that the national government cannot otherwise force the state to do is known as

(1) Equalization
(2) Elasticity
(3) Cross-over sanctions
(4) Fiscal federalism
(5) Revenue sharing.

3. The clause of the Constitution upon which Chief Justice John Marshall based his decision about the creation of a national bank in *McCulloch v. Maryland* was the

(1) Supremacy Clause
(2) Privileges and Immunities Clause
(3) Necessary and Proper Clause
(4) Full Faith and Credit Clause
(5) Interstate Commerce Clause.

4. The Supreme Court case that decided that the national government could not prohibit the shipment of goods manufactured by children who worked more than eight hours a day was

(1) *Hammer v. Dagenhart*
(2) *McCulloch v. Maryland*
(3) *United States v. Curtiss-Wright Export Corporation*
(4) *United States v. Darby*
(5) *Youngstown Sheet and Tube Company v. Sawyer.*

5. The Supreme Court minimized the importance of the Tenth Amendment and ended the "dual-federalism" interpretation of the Constitution in the case

(1) *Hammer v. Dagenhart*
(2) *McCulloch v. Maryland*
(3) *United States v. Curtiss-Wright Export Corporation*
(4) *United States v. Darby*
(5) *Youngstown Sheet and Tube Company v. Sawyer.*

14th edition

6. The War Against Terrorism, with its heightened security measures, will probably not be popular with people whose view of federalism is

   (1) Global
   (2) Self-centered
   (3) Civil libertarian
   (4) Pigmalian
   (5) Unitary

7. Supporters of NAFTA would embrace the _____ view of federalism.

   (1) Marble-cake
   (2) Fiscal
   (3) Unitary
   (3) Self-centered
   (4) Global

8. Supporters of the _____ view of federalism believe that this system of government will eventually evolve into one that is more efficient and more authoritarian.

   (1) Unitary
   (2) Fiscal
   (3) Global
   (4) Radical
   (5) Civil libertarian

9. Those who accept the _____ view of federalism look to the system for personal gain, especially monetary gain.

   (1) Global
   (2) Radical
   (3) Self-centered
   (4) Civil libertarian
   (5) Unitary

10. One or more of the following would be considered a mandate. Which one or ones?
    (1) The Supreme Court decision in *Brown* v. *Board of Education*, which ordered states to desegregate public schools.
    (2) Congress's passing a law requiring states to lower the speed limit to 55 m.p.h. or face losing federal highway funds.
    (3) Congress passing a law stating that certain chemicals can be dumped into rivers and streams in the United States as long as they don't exceed a preset limit.
    (4) The president's issuing an executive order to integrate the county's armed forces.
    (5) All

Fill-in-the-Blank Questions

Write the appropriate word or words in the blanks provided.

1. The _____ Act of 1916 prohibited the shipment of goods manufactured by children who worked more than eight hours a day.

2. The ability of a tax to grow with the economy without the need for legislative tax increases is called _____ .

3. What was the primary reason the authors of the Constitution created a federal system, instead of using a unitary system of government?
   _____

4. What questions was the Supreme Court asked to decide in the case *McCulloch v. Maryland?*

    (1) _____
    (2) _____

5. What did the Supreme Court decide in answer to those questions cited in #8 above?

    (1) _____
    (2) _____

True/False Questions

Write the correct response in the blanks provided.

1. A person who interprets the Constitution very narrowly and literally is said to be a strict constructionist. _____

2. Recent Supreme Court cases have seen the Court become more favorable toward the states' rights position on the issue of federalism. _____

3. The Supreme Court has ruled that the national government could not use cross-over sanctions. _____

Discussion Questions

Use your own paper to answer the following questions.

1. How did the 55 mile-an-hour speed limit demonstrate one of the criticisms of the grant-in-aid program?

2. What was meant by the term *state-dominated federalism?*

3. Explain Morton Grozens' characterization of American federalism today as a "marble cake."

4. Explain the significance of the Supreme Court case *McCulloch v. Maryland* as it relates to the concepts of states' rights and to federalism.

5. Does the constitutional principle contained in the Supremacy Clause support or undermine the principle of states' rights? Explain.

6. Explain the "necessary and proper" clause. Do you think this constitutional provision gives the national government too much power? Defend your answer.

Using Your Little Gray Cells

1. There has been a great deal of talk about balancing the budget of the federal government. One of the proposals is to add a constitutional amendment that would require the national government to balance its budget annually except during "national emergencies." Explain the drawbacks to such a proposal as stated.

2. Because of federalism, each state makes its own rules about who can marry whom, when, and under what conditions. The only national rules pertain to blatantly discriminatory practices in the past concerning race, for example. Should there be a uniform set of laws concerning such an important institution as marriage? Why or why not?

3. As a corollary to question #2 above, the state of Hawaii recently passed a law allowing same-sex marriages. Should homosexuals be required to travel all the way to Hawaii to marry or should the laws against same-sex marriages be struck down as unconstitutional as was done with laws denying people of different races to marry? Defend your position.

4. The national government still provides some tax money to the state or local governments for special projects. Poorer states usually get back more of the tax money collected in federal income taxes than do the richer states. Is this fair? Explain.

5. The role of the national government has changed since 1789. Do you think the writers of the Constitution would be pleased with balance of power between the national government and the state governments today? Explain.

6. How have the duties of law enforcement at the state-, local-, and national-government levels changed since September 11, 2002?

Chapter 4

14th edition

More important than winning the election, is governing the nation. That is the test of a political party —the acid, final test.

Adlai E. Stevenson
Democratic presidential candidate, 1952 and 1956

Chapter 5
POLITICAL PARTIES

Learning Objectives

After reading and studying the chapter on political parties, you should have a better understanding of the following:

1. The role of political parties in the United States;
2. The differences between political parties and pressures groups;
3. The nature and functions of democratic and nondemocratic parties;
4. Political party systems;
5. The two-party system in the United States;
6. The role of minor parties in the United States;
7. The nature and functions of state parties;
8. National and state party organization;
9. Political party tactics;
10. The merits and defects of American parties and party system;
11. What the future holds for American parties and party system.

Chapter Outline

I. Definition of Political Party
   A. Organized group which seeks to control governmental policy by occupying the positions of authority in government, either by force or through legitimate elections
   B. Includes
      1. Voters who support party with votes, financing, or work
      2. Government officials elected/appointed under party label
   C. Distinction between party officials and government officials particularly blurred in non-democratic countries

II. Comparison of Parties and Interest Groups
   A. Size
      1. Parties usually larger than interest groups
      2. Largest American labor union = 10 million members
      3. Largest American party = 30 to 40 million members
   B. Functions
      1. Parties: to win elections and control government
      2. Interest groups: to influence government
      3. Interest groups do not offer candidates themselves
   C. Scope of interest
      1. Parties broader in scope
      2. Interest groups narrower
   D. Ideology

1. Defined as person's way of interpreting world
   a. Conservatism
   b. Liberalism
   c. Militarism
   d. Communism
   e. Fascism
   f. Socialism
2. Major parties in United States non-ideological
   a. Democratic Party
   b. Republican Party
3. Most interest groups ideological
   a. National Rifle Association
   b. American Civil Liberties Union

III. Types of Political Parties
   A. Democratic
      1. Definition
         a. Open to anyone, not just privileged few
         b. Allow debate on party policies at all levels
      2. Types of democratic parties
         a. Ideological
            (1) Highly structured and organized
            (2) Unified
            (3) Disciplined
            (4) Example: British parties in House of Commons
         b. Non-ideological
            (1) Alliances of different groups
            (2) Not too structured
            (3) Not very unified
            (4) Not very disciplined
            (5) Examples
               • Democratic Party
               • Republican Party
   B. Non-democratic
      1. Definition
         a. Often open only to small number of people
         b. Debate usually takes place only at top levels of party
      2. Characterized as
         a. Always ideological
         b. Highly unified
         c. Highly organized
         d. Highly disciplined
      3. Examples
         a. Iraqi Ba'ath party
         b. Cuban Communist party
         c. German Nazi Party

14th edition

IV.   Functions of Democratic Parties
       A. Bring together differing interests
       B. Making demands on government
       C. Shaping public opinion
       D. Offering political alternatives
       E. Unifying different racial, ethnic, and interest groups
       F. Running the government
       G. Recruiting governmental personnel
       H. Criticizing and checking the party in power
       I. Orchestrating peaceful change
       J. Linking people to government

 V.   Political Party Systems
       A. Multi-party systems
           1. Three or more major political parties
           2. Favorite among democracies
           3. Can produce instability in government
           3. Examples
               a. France
               b. Italy
       B. Two-party systems
           1. Two major political parties
           2. Usually non-ideological or less ideological
           3. Governments tend to be more stable than in multi-party
               systems
           4. Examples
               a. United States
               b. Canada
               c. Great Britain
       C. One-party systems
           1. One major political party
           2. Opposition frequently not tolerated
           3. Usually found in dictatorships
           4. Usually ideological
           5. Examples
               a. Cuba--non-democratic
               b. People's Republic of China--non-democratic

VI.   The Two-Party System in the United States
       A. Tradition
           1. Parties developed over ratification of Constitution
           2. British had two-party system
       B. Democratic: considered "un-American" not to have choices
       C. Single-member election districts
           1. Person who gets most votes wins
           2. Seats in legislative branch not awarded proportionally

57

Chapter 5

3. Presidential election requires majority of electoral vote
4. Thus, minor parties have difficulty pulling enough votes

VII. Impact of the Two-Party System
   A. Majority government at all levels
      1. No coalition governments
      2. "Watchdog" role for party that doesn't win presidency
   B. Alliance nature of parties: alliances of many differing groups
   C. Similar constituencies of parties
      1. Same kinds of people found in both parties
      2. All shades of political spectrum in both parties
   D. Non-ideological parties
      1. Parties agree on general principles
      2. But can differ on how to achieve goals
   E. Lack of significant minor parties
      1. Minor parties usually exist
      2. But offer no serious challenge to major parties usually
   F. Role of "watchdog"
      1. Refers to party which does not control presidency
      2. Loyal to government but reserves right to criticize other party

IX. Minor Parties
   A. Rarely elect their candidates
   B. Functions
      1. New ideas
         a. Anti-Masons developed national convention for nominating president and vice-president
         b. Populist Party advocated direct election of Senators and women's right to vote
         c. Socialist Party advocated unemployment compensation, old-age pensions, workman's compensation, and graduated income tax
      2. Possible balance of power in close elections
         a. Pull votes usually from one party
         b. Examples
            (1) 1912: Progressives possibly caused election of
            (2) 1968: Republicans feared American Independent Party would cause election of Democrat
         c. If no presidential candidate wins electoral majority, then
            (1) President selected by House of Representatives
            (2) Vice president selected by Senate
      3. Expression of minority opinion
         a. Major parties unlikely to champion causes opposed by
         b. Minor parties ideological and can afford to champion such causes

14th edition

X.   State Parties
   A. Functions: essentially same as national parties
   B. Nature
       1. Not duplicates of national parties
       2. Actually affiliates of national parties
       3. Possess high degree of independence
       4. Receive no instruction from national parties concerning candidates or policy

   XI. National Party Organization
   A. National party organization rather loose
   B. National Convention
       1. Theoretically supreme legislative organ of national party
       2. Functions
           a. Nominates presidential and vice-presidential candidates
               (1) Vice-presidential candidates actually selected by presidential nominee
               (2) Vice-presidential nominee often nominated by acclamation
           b. Serves as agency of compromise
           c. Has committee to draft platform
           d. Helps to raise money for party's nominee
           e. Tries to create or solidify strong loyalty to party among
           f. Tries to impress new voters and independent voters
           e. Rising numbers of independent voters
       3. Number and selection of delegates
           a. Varies from state to state and party to party
           b. Selection by presidential primary elections, or party caucuses, or by state party conventions
           c. Presidential primaries very popular
   C. National Committee
       1. Main party organization at national level
       2. Functions
           a. Conducts party business when Convention not in session
           b. Offers advice and assistance during presidential campaign
           c. Selects location and dates of next convention
           d. Helps raise funds for party's candidates
           e. Fills vacancies on party's ticket if they occur after
       3. Composition
           a. One man and one woman from each state
           b. Usually prominent people
   D. National Chairperson
       1. Most powerful person on National Committee
       2. Functions

59

Chapter 5

14th edition

    a. Organizes and conducts presidential campaign
    b. Keeps in touch with state and local party leaders
    c. Helps raise money for campaign
    d. Tries to keep party unified behind candidates
    e. Prepares for next election
    f. Serves as spokesperson for party if its candidate did not win presidency
    g. Helps president (if party's candidate won) in "controlling" party
    h. Helps president (if party's candidate won) dispense patronage
    i. Often receives patronage position himself/herself

XII. State Party Organization
    A. State Committee: varying degrees of authority over actions of party and party members
    B. County Committee: usually plays very significant role in local matters
    C. Precinct Captain
        1. Exists where strong party organization exists locally
        2. In charge of voting district usually consisting of 1000 voters or less
        3. Responsibilities
            a. Getting party's supporters to vote
            b. Distributing campaign materials
            c. Keeping informed about what is going on politically in precinct
    D. Mass media had negative impact on party organization

XIII. Political Party Tactics
    A. Goal of party: to win elections so as to control public policy making
    B. Electioneering
        1. Refers to those things parties do to get candidates elected
        2. Types of electioneering
            a. Propaganda
                (1) Use of words or pictures to persuade voters
                (2) Television very prominent tool today
            b. Organization
                (1) Very important in winning elections
                (2) The better organized party is, the better its chances of success
            c. Patronage
                (1) The promise of government jobs
                (2) Not as prominent today because of merit system
                (3) Still many jobs subject to patronage
            d. Illegalities
                (1) Buying votes
                (2) Threats of violence

60

Chapter 5

XIV. Evaluation of United States Parties and Party System
  A. No ideological consistency
  B. Party balancing act trying to please conflicting interests
  C. Lack of party responsibility, long-range planning, and consistency

Important Terms

Federalist Number 10
Multi-member district
Non-democratic parties
Non-ideological parties
Proportional representation
Multi-party system
One-party system
Coalition government
Single-member district
National Chairperson
National Committee

Political party
Ideology
Ideological parties
Presidential primaries
National Convention
Two-party system
Anti-Federalists
Federalist Party
Democratic parties
Patronage
Focus group

Precinct
Electioneering
Precinct captain
Federalists
Acclamation
Platform
Propaganda
Exit polling
State Committee
Minor party

Multiple Choice Questions
Circle the number of the correct answer.

1. In *Federalist Number 10,* James Madison warned against the dangers of

    (1) dictatorship
    (2) interest groups
    (3) monarchy
    (4) a Bill of Rights
    (5) a strong military.

2. The Federalists were people who

    (1) supported the Bill of Rights
    (2) supported ratification of the new constitution
    (3) did not support ratification of the new constitution
    (4) supported strong political parties
    (5) did not support strong political parties.

3. Any organized group of people who seek to control governmental policy by occupying the positions of authority in the government, either by force or through legitimate elections, is called a (an)

(1) political party
(2) interest group
(3) faction
(4) pressure group
(5) all of the above.

4. One of the following is not true of political parties in the United States:

(1) political parties are usually larger than interest groups
(2) political parties usually have a narrower focus of interest than interest groups
(3) the main function of political parties is to run candidates who win public office
(4) major political parties are usually not ideological
(5) political parties at the national level are coalitions of interest groups and state parties.

5. Liberalism and conservatism are examples of

(1) political parties
(2) interest groups
(3) pressure groups
(4) ideologies
(5) both #1 and #4.

6. The broad category of political parties that are open to anyone, not just a privileged few, and that allow debate on party policies at all levels of party activity is

(1) authoritarian parties
(2) democratic parties
(3) non-democratic parties
(4) ideological parties
(5) non-ideological parties.

7. The House of Commons refers to

(1) the college cafeteria
(2) a fashion boutique
(3) a place where the poor can get food and shelter
(4) the legislative branch of the state of Illinois
(5) a part of the British Parliament.

14th edition

8. The broad category of political parties that usually are not open to everyone, where party policy matters are normally decided by top party leaders is called

    (1) authoritarian parties
    (2) democratic parties
    (3) non-democratic parties
    (4) ideological parties
    (5) non-ideological parties.

9. One of the following is <u>not</u> a characteristic of ideological parties:

    (1) loosely organized
    (2) highly structured
    (3) highly disciplined
    (4) highly unified
    (5) found in both democratic and non-democratic countries.

10. The political parties found in the British House of Commons are examples of

    (1) democratic parties
    (2) nondemocratic parties
    (3) ideological parties
    (4) nonideological parties
    (5) both #1 and #3.

11. The two major parties in the United States are examples of

    (1) democratic parties
    (2) non-democratic parties
    (3) ideological parties
    (4) non-ideological parties
    (5) both #1 and #4.

12. One of the following is <u>not</u> true of the two major political parties in the United States: they are

    (1) loosely organized
    (2) made up of many different groups of people
    (3) highly disciplined
    (4) loosely structured
    (5) generally non-ideological.

14th edition

13. The Communist Party in Cuba is an example of a (an)

    (1) democratic party
    (2) non-democratic party
    (3) ideological party
    (4) non-ideological party
    (5) both #2 and #3.

14. One of the following countries has a one-party system:

    (1) France
    (2) Canada
    (3) Cuba
    (4) Italy
    (5) Great Britain.

15. One of the following countries has a two-party system:

    (1) France
    (2) Russia
    (3) Cuba
    (4) Italy
    (5) Great Britain.

16. One or more of the following countries have a multi-party system:

    (1) France
    (2) Italy
    (3) Great Britain
    (4) all--#1, #2, and #3
    (5) only #1 and #2.

17. One of the following is not a characteristic of some multi-party systems:

    (1) highly stable governments
    (2) frequent coalition governments
    (3) usually occurring in parliamentary systems with proportional representation in the legislative branch
    (4) found in most democratic countries today
    (5) usually has ideological parties.

18. One of the following is <u>not</u> a characteristic of two-party systems:

    (1) parties are usually non-ideological
    (2) parties usually survive longer than parties in multi-party systems
    (3) parties are leader oriented
    (4) parties are alliances of many groups
    (5) parties undisciplined.

19. One of the following is <u>not</u> a characteristic of one-party systems:

    (1) parties are usually non-democratic
    (2) parties are usually ideological
    (3) parties are not leader oriented
    (4) party organization and structure often overlap with government organization and structure
    (5) opposition parties are not usually tolerated.

20. The first political party in the United States was the

    (1) Democratic-Republican Party
    (2) Whig Party
    (3) Republican Party
    (4) Federalist Party
    (5) Anti-Federalist Party.

21. The second political party to form in the United States was the

    (1) Democratic-Republican Party
    (2) Whig Party
    (3) Republican Party
    (4) Federalist Party
    (5) Anti-Federalist Party.

22. The <u>major</u> political party which grew out of the Anti-Federalists was the

    (1) Democratic-Republican Party
    (2) Whig Party
    (3) Republican Party
    (4) Federalist Party
    (5) American Party.

14th edition

23. The minor party that came up with the idea of nominating presidential and vice-presidential candidates at national conventions was the

    (1) Anti-Mason Party
    (2) Populist Party
    (3) Free Soil Party
    (4) Greenback Party
    (5) Communist Party.

24. The first minor party to advocate direct election of senators was the

    (1) Anti-Mason Party
    (2) Populist Party
    (3) Free Soil Party
    (4) Greenback Party
    (5) Communist Party.

25. If a vice-presidential candidate has been nominated for that office at the national convention by a voice vote, he/she is said to have been nominated by

    (1) viva voca
    (2) vox populi
    (3) acclamation
    (4) affirmation
    (5) none of the above.

26. The party organization that selects the site and dates of the political party conventions of the major parties in the United States is the

    (1) National Committee
    (2) state governors
    (3) Credentials Committee
    (4) Platform Resolutions Committee
    (5) Convention Committee.

27. The party organization that fills vacancies on the party's presidential and vice-presidential ticket if they occur after the convention has adjourned is the

    (1) National Committee
    (2) Candidate Replacement Committee
    (3) Credentials Committee
    (4) Platform Resolutions Committee
    (5) Convention Committee.

14th edition

28. The party organization that conducts party business when the convention is not in session is the

    (1) National Committee
    (2) Convention Committee
    (3) Credentials Committee
    (4) Platform Resolutions Committee
    (5) Board of Directors of the two major political parties.

29. Doing all the things political parties need to do to win an election is referred to as

    (1) propaganda
    (2) patronage
    (3) electioneering
    (4) image-making
    (5) market segmentation.

30. The use of words or pictures to convey the party's ideas to the voters so that the party can win the election is referred to specifically as

    (1) propaganda
    (2) patronage
    (3) electioneering
    (4) image-making
    (5) market segmentation.

31. The Anti-Federalists were

    (1) The first political party in the U.S.
    (2) The second political party in the U.S.
    (3) Supported ratification of the Constitution of 1789
    (4) Made up of plantation and business owners.
    (5) Opposed ratification of the Constitution of 1789.

Fill-in-the-Blank Questions

Write the appropriate word or words in the blanks provided.

1. A statement of the political party's program and ideals is called its

    _____ .

2. The functions of minor parties in a two-party system are
    (1) _____
    (2) _____
    (3) _____

14th edition

3. The three most common methods of selecting delegates to the national conventions are

   (1) _____

   (2) _____

   (3) _____

4. The most popular type of party system in democratic countries is the _____-party system.

5. In a multi-member election district, _____ representation exists in the legislative branch of government.

6. What three reasons can be given for the two-party system's existence in the United States?

   (1) _____

   (2) _____

   (3) _____

7. The practice or rewarding faithful party members by appointing them to various positions in government is called _____ .

8. The most powerful person on the National Committee is the

   _____ .

9. A political party system that has only one major political party is called a (an) _____ party system.

10. A political party system that has only two major political parties is called a (an) _____ party system.

11. A political party system that has three or more major political parties is called a (an) _____ party system.

12. A (An) _____ is a local party official who is responsible for getting the party's supporters to vote, distributing campaign materials, and generally keeping informed about what is going on politically in his/her voting district.

13. A way of interpreting the world around us, making sense out of it, or organizing it is called a (an) _____ .

14th edition

14. In democratic countries, what *groups of people* are included in political parties?

    (1) _____

    (2) _____

    (3) _____

15. A (An) _____ is a voting district consisting of about 1000 voters or less.

True/False Questions

Write the correct answer in the blanks provided.

1. Party leaders can never be government officials at the same time. _____

2. There are no minor parties found in either one-party systems or in two-party systems. _____

3. State political parties are merely branches of the national parties; they don't have much control of their own activities. _____

4. The better the party organization, the easier it is for the party to win. _____

5. American major political parties are ideologically consistent in their views on both domestic and foreign policy. _____

6. American major political parties are well known for their ability to make long-range plans for governing. _____

7. Because the United States has a two-party system, state parties and national parties rarely differ on issues. _____

8. When people vote for a party's nominees for state offices, they always vote for the same party's nominees at the national level. _____

9. Political parties in the United States usually have difficulty raising as much money as interest groups do. _____

10. The major parties in the United States are so far apart ideologically that they argue about fundamentals. _____

11. Because state party organization in the United States is strong everywhere, most precincts have a precinct captain. _____

12. One-party systems can be found *only* in dictatorships. _____

14th edition

13. Political parties and interest groups are identical except that parties run candidates and interest groups don't. _____

14. The national nominating conventions meet every two years to nominate candidates for the House of Representatives, the Senate, the president and the vice president. _____

15. The U.S. has proportional representation in Congress and single member districts. _____

16. Coalition governments are unlikely to occur in countries with two-party systems and parliamentary governments. _____

17. Exit polling has proved to be a reliable predictor of the outcome of presidential elections. _____

18. Party activists (elites) from both major U.S. parties tend to be more ideological than the party voters. _____

Discussion Questions

Use your own paper to answer the following questions.

1. Compare single-member election districts to multi-member election districts.

2. Explain how single-member election districts discourage the formation or continuation of minor parties.

3. What did former Alabama Governor George Wallace mean by his statement that there is not a "dime's worth of difference" between the two major parties in the United States?

4. Define *ideology* and explain its role in the two major parties in the United States.

5. How do American political parties differ from interest groups in the United States?

14th edition

Using Your Little Gray Cells

1. Write a report summarizing the reasons for the decline in party loyalty over the past years. (There are many sources for this information in libraries. One that you might find useful is Carl Everett Ladd's *Where Have All the Voters Gone.*

2. It has often been said that the Democratic Party became a "mass party" or a "party of the people" when Andrew Jackson was elected President. Write a report on why the election of Jackson is said to have marked the beginning of this characteristic of the Democratic Party. As a conclusion to your paper, is this "people's-party" image part of the party's propaganda; do you think the Democratic Party today deserves this title? Give reasons for your answer.

3. Find out who currently serves from your state on the National Committee of the Democratic Party and who serves on the National Committee of the Republican Party.

4. Find out how the Republican Party came to be referred to as the "Grand Old Party" (GOP).

5. The patronage system was dealt a severe blow in 1980 in the Supreme Court case *Branti v. Finkel* 445 U.S. 507 (1980). What were the facts of the case and what did the Supreme Court rule?

6. Give a report on the history of the two major political parties in Great Britain: the Labour Party and the Conservative Party.

7. In groups of three or four, assume you are all delegates to a Democratic or Republican party convention who have also been asked to serve on the party's Platform and Resolutions Committee. Your group's task is to propose a "plank" in the platform. Select some issue you think is worthy of consideration--a problem and a proposed solution. Write your group's ideas in the following format: (1) state the problem; (2) summarize the solution and why you think this solution will work; (3) summarize why you think your proposal would appeal to the voters and which voters would it appeal to most.

14th edition

CHAPTER 6
INTEREST GROUPS
THE POLITICS OF NUMBERS

AMERICAN ASSOCIATION OF RETIRED PERSONS

AMERICAN HEART ASSOCIATION

MOVE AMERICA FORWARD

GODLESS AMERICANS POLITICAL ACTION COMMITTEE

Jewish Anti-Defamation League

PEANUT GROWERS ASSOCIATION

Flat Earth Society

Learning Objectives

After reading and studying the chapter on interest groups in the text,
you should have a better understanding of the following:

1. Why the United States is considered a polyarchical democracy;
2. Why people join groups;
3. What interest groups are and how they are formed;
4. The types of interest groups;
5. What interest groups do and the methods they use to achieve their goals;
6. Why interest groups are useful;
7. The problems connected with interest groups;
8. The future of interest group activity.

Chapter Outline

I. Group Democracy
   A. Also referred to as pluralist democracy or polyarchical democracy
   B. Definition: system of democracy based on groups rather than on individual members of society
   C. Most group membership voluntary
      1. Allows individual expression of opinion on issues within group context
      2. Monetary benefits
      3. Social contacts
   D. Some membership required in some places
      1. State bar associations
      2. Labor unions

II. Definition of Interest Group
   A. Organization of people who share common goals and concerns and seek to influence public policy
   B. Also called pressure groups

III. Formation of Interest Groups
   A. Potential interest groups: any unorganized groups who possess some commonalty
   B. Real interest groups: organized groups who possess some commonalty and seek to influence public policy

IV. Categories of Interest Groups
  A. Economic
      1. Revolve around type of work person does to earn living
      2. Types of work-based interest groups
          a. Business groups
              (1) Chamber of Commerce
              (2) National Association of Manufacturers
              (3) Business Roundtable
              (4) National Federation of Independent Businesses
          b. Labor groups
              (1) Knights of Labor
                  (a) First successful labor union in U.S.
                  (b) Highest membership: 700,000
              (2) Labor unions weakened
                  (a) Membership decline
                      •   Still about 16 million members
                      •   2/3 belong to AFL-CIO
                  (b) Reasons for decline
                      •   Unions failed to cope effectively with change
                      •   Unions have a tarnished public image
                      •   Traditional labor allies gone
                      •   Possibly unions too interested in maintaining higher wages for the bulk of members at the expense of recruiting younger workers and minority workers
          c. Agricultural groups
              (1) Protest organizations
              (2) Multipurpose organizations
              (3) Single issue organizations
          d. Professional groups
              (1) American Medical Association--physicians
              (2) American Bar Association--attorneys
              (3) National Education Association--educators
  B. Non-economic interest groups
      1. Formed around something other than the way a person makes a living; e.g., race, sex, age, ideology, issues
      2. Examples
          a. NOW
          b. League of Women Voters
          c. American Association of University Women
          d. Common Cause
          e. Wilderness Society
          f. Sierra Club
          g. Consumers' Union
          h. Physicians for Social Responsibility

74
Chapter 6
14th edition

    i. Muslim interest groups
- Council on American-Islamic Relations
- Muslim Public Affairs Council
- American Muslim Council

  C. New Agency and New Clientele
    1. Department of Homeland Security
    2. Created huge new lobbying clientele
    3. Examples
      a. American Federation of Government Employees
      b. National Emergency Management Association
      c. American Chemistry Council
      d. American Association of Port Authorities

VI. Interest Group Tactics
  A. Propaganda
    1. Use of words and images to persuade people to respond in a particular way
    2. Tries to create favorable public image for group
    3. Tries to create support for group cause
    4. Example: institutionalized advertising
  B. Lobbying
    1. Communication between group/group members and public officials
    2. Types of lobbying
      (a) Direct
        (1) One-on-one meetings with government officials or
        (2) Testifying at hearings
      (b) Indirect
        (1) Many companies involved in organizing indirect lobbying campaigns for groups
- Consulting
- Strategic planning
- Signature gathering
- Telephone and direct mail contacts

        (2) Expensive but effective
  C. Electioneering
    1. Helping candidates get elected to office
    2. Less control by parties today; more by candidates
    3. Radio/TV play large role
    4. PACs: raise and distribute money for various campaigns
      (a) Types of PACs
        (1) Connected
- Have sponsoring organizations
- Usually corporations and interest groups
- Corporate PACs = around 1800

- Union PACs = around 350
- Other groups = 1000

    (2) Non-connected
- Do not have sponsoring agency
- Number about 1100

  (b) Total number exceeds 40,000

D. Litigation
1. Law suits
2. Courts more passive than executive or legislative branches
   a. Courts must have disputes brought to them before they can act
   b. Courts have option to hear the case or not
   c. Courts follow more prescribed rules and procedures
3. Types of litigation
   a. Bringing suits on behalf of members
   b. Class action lawsuits
      (1) Joining with others in a lawsuit
      (2) May involve thousands of people--a "class" of people who are suing
   c. *Amicus curiae* briefs
      (1) Filed with permission of the court
      (2) Written legal argument "for" or "against" the issue before the court

E. Violence
1. Illegal use of force
2. Used by some groups in United States
3. Examples
   a. Ku Klux Klan
   b. American Nazi Party
   c. Aryan Nation
   d. American Front
   e. Nation of Islam
   f. Animal Liberation Brigade
4. Not used by most interest groups because
   a. Most Americans do not believe violence is acceptable
   b. Interest groups have peaceful access to government

VII. The Future of Interest Groups
A. Groups are important part of political system in US
B. Interest groups ideological
C. Interest group activity not likely to decrease in future
D. Major controversy concerning PACs money

14th edition

Important Terms

Group democracy
Real interest group
National Education
   Association
Muslim Public Affairs
   Council
Grassroots lobbying
Business Roundtable
Connected PAC
American Farm Bureau
   Federation
American Nazi Party
Chamber of Commerce
American Muslim Council
American Federation of
   Government Employees
American Association of
   Port Authorities

Aryan Nation
Potential interest group
Non-economic interest
   group
National Association of
   Manufacturers
United Farm Workers
AFL-CIO
Non-connected PAC
National Farmers
   Organization
American Bar Association
Political action committee
Litigation
National Emergency
   Management Association
527 Groups

Propaganda
Interest group
American Agriculture
   Movement
American Medical
   Association
Direct lobbying
Common Cause
Ku Klux Klan
Council on American-
   Islamic Relations
Lobbying
Electioneering
Unisys
American Chemical
   Council

Multiple Choice Questions

Circle the number of the correct answer.

1. One of the following is an economic interest group:

    (1) American Farm Bureau Federation
    (2) Mothers Against Drunk Drivers
    (3) NAACP
    (4) American Association of Retired Persons
    (5) Boy Scouts of America.

2. Which one of the following is **not** a correct reason for the decline of labor unions?

    (1) Unions' public image has been tarnished by scandals
    (2) Membership in unions has declined
    (3) Unions have not coped well with societal changes
    (4) Labor unions are illegal in many states
    (5) Many of labor's traditional friends have passed from the political scene.

14th edition

3. When pressure groups help candidates get elected to office, they are engaging in a tactic called

    (1) propaganda
    (2) lobbying
    (3) electioneering
    (4) pressure group formation
    (5) recruitment.

4. The use of words or images in order to persuade the public to think or act in a certain way is called

    (1) recruitment
    (2) electioneering
    (3) lobbying
    (4) pressure group formation
    (5) propaganda.

5. Groups that were formed to get around laws severely limiting campaign donations by labor unions and corporations are called

    (1) real interest groups
    (2) political action committees
    (3) trade associations
    (4) pressure groups
    (5) campaign committees.

6. An interest group activity involving personal contact with government officials by those representing interest groups is called

    (1) lobbying
    (2) electioneering
    (3) propaganda
    (4) picketing
    (5) recruitment.

7. Approximately how many *connected* PACs are there today in the United States?

    (1) 3150
    (2) 1500
    (3) 1800
    (4) 350
    (5) 1000

Chapter 6

8. Approximately how many **non-connected** PACs are there today in the United States?

   (1) 1700
   (2) 1500
   (3) 2000
   (4) 1100
   (5) 350

9. PACs donate the largest share of their money to candidates for the

   (1) U.S. House of Representatives
   (2) presidency
   (3) U.S. Senate
   (4) state legislatures
   (5) judgeships

10. One of the most widely recognized, public-interest pressure groups is

   (1) NOW
   (2) AMA
   (3) AARP
   (4) NAACP
   (5) Common Cause

Fill-in-the-Blank Questions

Write the correct word or words in the blanks provided.

1. The United States is said to have a _____ democracy because the governmental system functions primarily with groups.

2. Americans tend to join groups <u>voluntarily (meaning because they want to, not forced to)</u> for a number of reasons. List these reasons.

   (1) _____
   (2) _____
   (3) _____

3. Another name for an interest group is _____ group.

4. A (an) _____ is an organized group of people who seek to influence public policy.

5. Unorganized groups of people with certain common characteristics or interests are said to be _____ interest groups.

79
Chapter 6

6. A (an) _____ interest group is one whose common interest revolves how a person makes his/her living.

7. When an interest group goes to court and sues, it is said to be involved in an interest group tactic known as _____ .

8. The four categories of economic interest groups are

(1) _____   (3) _____
(2) _____   (4) _____

9. Give one example of economic interest groups for each of the four categories named in question #8.

(1) _____   (3) _____
(2) _____   (4) _____

10. Groups that are formed around something other than the way a person makes his/her living are called _____ pressure groups.

11. The five tactics used by interest groups to achieve their goals are

(1) _____
(2) _____
(3) _____
(4) _____
(5) _____

12. _____ PACs are those that do not have a sponsoring organization and frequently are highly ideological.

13. The _____ , the _____ , and the _____ are three pressure groups that have frequently utilized violence as a method of attempting to achieve their goals.

14. _____ lobbying includes such activities as one-on-one meetings between lobbyists and members of the government or their staffs, testifying at legislative or administrative hearings, or bringing a class action lawsuit before the federal courts.

15. The BITE BACK program of the National Restaurant Association is part of its _____ lobbying efforts.

16. _____ PACs are those that have a sponsoring organization that may pay operating and fund-raising expenses.

14th edition

17. Both _____ and _____ are the category of groups that usually form sponsored PACs.

18. A type of litigation in which an interest group would join with others in some court action is called a (an) _____.

19. A written argument filed by interest groups or by individuals who are not parties to a case but who are interested in the outcome and wish to "put their two cents worth" before the judge is called a (an) _____ brief.

20. Among the fastest growing interest groups in the United States at the national level represent _____ and _____, who are well funded and typically support Democratic candidates.

True/False

Write the correct answer in the blanks provided.

1. Farm groups are often very different from one another even though the issues they address are all related to agriculture. _____

2. One of the major problems facing physicians today is the cost of medical malpractice insurance. _____

3. The AMA has had much influence on legislation such as Medicare. _____

4. The Aryan Nation is an interest group that represents the interests of majority people (Caucasians) in such traditional ways as filing lawsuits, lobbying, and electioneering. _____

5. Only powerful, well-financed interest groups such as the Business Roundtable actually have any influence over public policy. _____

6. Ethnic groups and religious groups rarely form interest groups. _____

7. Sometimes government agencies will lobby other government agencies. _____

14th edition

Discussion Questions

Use your own paper to answer the following questions.

1. Compare and contrast the U.S. Chamber of Commerce and the Business Roundtable.

2. Why has the influence of labor unions declined in the last decade? What do you think labor unions should do in order to rekindle their influence?

3. How are interest groups an integral part of the U.S. political system?

4. Why has violence as a pressure group tactic been relatively unsuccessful in the United States?

5. Although many people think business pressure groups stick together and support each other all the time, this is not always the case. Under what circumstances might the American Petroleum Institute and the National Automobile Dealers Association come into conflict? (Think about this one in terms of the price of oil.)

6. Explain how "grassroots" lobbying works and why it may be more successful than traditional lobbying done by paid lobbyists.

7. Define a 527 group. What do you see as problems with the functioning of these groups and elections in the United States?

Using Your Little Gray Cells

1. Look in magazines and find an ad for the National Rifle Association or any other interest group, for example, child sponsorship groups. Bring it to class and show the class what messages, both obvious and not so obvious, does the organization want to send to the public.

2. Write a report or make an oral presentation on Ralph Nader, a well-known lobbyist for consumer interests. What successes and failures has he had? What tactics does he use?

3. Search the Internet and library sources to find press releases or speeches by Sheik Hisham Kabbani. Give a report to the class about why he thinks Muslim extremists have undue influence in the Arab community in the United States.

4. "Love Canal": Read the following story. Then either individually or in groups, answer the questions at the end of the story.

It is 1970. Your name is Lois Gibbs. You live with your spouse and children in the Love Canal area of Niagara Falls, New York. Love Canal is a quiet, well-kept subdivision of reasonably priced homes. Recently a strong odor has filled the air; sores and blisters have appeared for no apparent reason on the children and their pets; the soil has begun to ooze some colored substances, and the ground has begun to develop large sink holes. In addition, basement walls and floors of houses in the area have begun to experience a black gooey seepage; the once nicely landscaped yards look as if someone had used vegetation killer on them; people are getting sick; miscarriages have increased dramatically, and many children are born with birth defects. When an insecticide was discovered later in fish in Lake Ontario and traced to a dump site near Love Canal, the residents thought they had found the reason for all their problems. This particular canal, begun in 1890, was never completed and was eventually purchased by the Hooker Electrochemical Company, which used the canal as a dump site. Between 1942 and 1952, the company, using accepted procedures for disposing of chemicals at that time, dumped 21,000 tons of chemical wastes in the canal. By 1953, the canal was full and covered over. Then the company sold the land (including the dump site) to the Niagara Falls School Board. By the terms of the sale, Hooker was exempted from any liability resulting from chemical wastes. In 1955, the school board built a school on part of the land and sold the rest to a developer who constructed several hundred homes on the site.

In 1972, the Commissioner of Health for the State of New York issued the following statement: "A review of all of the available evidence has convinced me of the existence of a great and imminent peril to the health and safety of the general public residing at or near the said site as a result of exposure to toxic substances emanating from the site." Initial studies of the area revealed ten compounds, seven of them cancer producing, while later studies documented 200 chemicals at the site. The Commissioner recommended that pregnant women, as well as children less than two years old, temporarily reside elsewhere and that all residents stay out of their basements.

You are Lois Gibbs, an ordinary person, who has never really been involved in politics. Write an *essay* on the following pages in which you answer the questions below. Pay attention to the organization, style, and spelling in your essay. Use the next page to write out an **essay** addressing the following questions.

- What would you do in this situation?
- Should the government be involved? If so, which one or ones?
- Is anyone responsible for these conditions? If so, who and why?
- List as many alternative solutions to the problem as you can think of. Then choose the one you think best.
- What are your reasons for your choice?
- How would you implement your option?

_____

_____

_____

_____

_____

_____

_____

_____

_____

_____

_____

_____

_____

_____

_____

_____

_____

_____

_____

_____

_____

_____

Internet Assignments

1. Virtually all major interest groups have Internet sites through which they hope to recruit members and get their positions across to the public. Of these interest groups, Washington insiders usually rank the American Association of Retired Persons as the most powerful. Go to the AARP Web site located at http://www.aarp.org. Evaluate how well the group accomplishes these two goals by citing specific examples.

2. Mothers Against Drunk Driving is well known throughout the country for its stance on the issue of drunk driving. Go to its Internet site located at http://www.madd.org. What specific changes in the law does this group now advocate? What is your evaluation of these proposals?

3. In the last four decades, there has been a raging debate about the use of tobacco products in the United States. There are numerous Internet sites on this controversy. The following site provides links to many of them: http://www.tobaccoresolution.com. Prepare a report using these sites on the pros and cons of banning the use of tobacco in the United States.

Public opinion is stronger than the legislature and nearly as strong as the Ten Commandments.

Charles Dudley Warner, 1829-1900

Chapter 7
Public Opinion

Learning Objectives

After reading and studying the chapter on public opinion in the text, you should have a better understanding of the following:

1. The meaning and importance of political socialization;
2. How political socialization occurs;
3. The sources of political socialization;
4. The function and importance of public opinion, particularly in democratic societies;
5. The relationship between political socialization and public opinion;
6. The factors that influence the formation of public opinion;
7. How and why public opinion is measured;
8. The meaning and significance of the intensity and stability of public opinion and the factors which influence these characteristics;
9. The correspondence or lack of it between public opinion and public policy.

Chapter Outline

I. Political Socialization
   A. The process by which we acquire our political attitudes
   B. Types of political socialization
      1. Direct
         a. Process by which political attitudes and ideas are
         b. Examples
            (1) Parent telling child to respect rights of others
            (2) Teacher teaching patriotic songs
      2. Indirect
         a. Process by which political attitudes and ideas are learned by observing others
         b. Examples
            (1) Child observes parents voting
            (2) Child observes parents reading newspapers
   C. Sources (Agents) of political socialization
      1. Family
         a. Most important
         b. Day-care centers may act as substitute "family"
      2. Schools
         a. Have children for long periods of time
         b. Teach democratic way of life
         c. Second major source of political socialization
      3. Peers

        a. Like family, they "reward" for "right" thinking and "punish" for "wrong" thinking
        b. Peers usually do not override influence of family except in areas of particular relevance to group
        c. Gangs qualify as peer influences
    4. Clergy
        a. Teach fairness, honesty, hard work, and loyalty connected to a deity
        b. Clergy's influence dependent on involvement of individual
    5. Mass media
        a. Adults get most political information from television
        b. Attitudes can be taught indirectly through television
           (1) Positive attitude toward space program through "Star Trek"
           (2) Positive attitude toward police through shows like *CSI* and *Law and Order*
           (3) Negative toward government: *Fahrenheit 9/11*
           (4) Effects of mass media both direct and indirect

II. Public Opinion
    A. Definition
       1. Beliefs expressed by a relatively large number of people on matters of public concern
       2. Different from, but connected to, political socialization
         a. Political socialization = <u>how</u> people learn to think
         b. Public opinion = <u>what</u> people think politically
       3. Latent opinions
         a. Unexpressed public opinions
         b. May become public opinion (expressed opinion) when issue becomes important to individual
    B. Factors Influencing Public Opinion
       1. Same factors (or some variation of them) that influence political socialization also influence public opinion
       2. Opinion leaders
         a. People who have more than usual influence on opinion of others
         b. Examples
           (1) Family member
           (2) Clergy
           (3) Teacher
           (4) Movie star
           (5) Rock singer
           (6) Newscaster
           (7) Politician
       3. Socioeconomic background
         a. Combination of family background, educational level, level of income, etc.
         b. Class one comes from "colors" opinions

4. Peers
   a. Difficult to disagree with friends and associates
   b. Unknown whether person accepts opinions of friends or whether person picks friends because they hold same opinions as he/she does
5. Clergy
   a. Especially influential on people who are heavily involved
   b. Even if expressed opinion disagreed with, person at least forced to think about issue
6. Mass media
   a. Media cannot cause most people to their change minds
   b. Tend to reinforce existing opinions--"filter effect"
   c. Only when person approaches issue with relatively open mind can media have real influence on opinion
   d. Media persuasion more effective when there is someone with whom to discuss subject
   e. Also more effective when opinion leader used by media
C. Significance of public opinion
   1. Traditional view
      a. Public opinion generated by people
      b. Public opinion is driving force for public policy, especially in democracies
   2. Elitist view
      a. Public opinion among masses generated by elites who control large segments of society and government
         (1) Formal elites = government office holders/policy makers
         (2) Informal elites = those behind the scenes who influence the policy makers
      b. Masses merely propagandized by elites
      c. Both views have some validity depending on issue
D. Measuring public opinion
   1. Public opinion polls
      a. Most reliable measure
      b. Scientific polls developed by Roper and Gallup
      c. Problems
         (1) Margin of error
         (2) Wording of questions
         (3) Respondent's lack of knowledge
         (4) Forced opinion
         (5) Contradictory opinions
         (6) Lying
   2. Polling and Elections
      a. Not particularly reliable method
         (1) Elections usually involve many issues of varying importance to individuals
         (2) Candidates often do not take clear stands on issues

(3) Significant number of people do not vote
(4) Some people vote for candidates for reasons unrelated to issues
- b. Projection Polls in the 1996 Presidential Election
- c. Election of 2000
  - (1) Networks kept changing their projected winner
  - (2) Over use of exit polls
  - (3) Recommendation to abandon exit polls
- d. Exit Polls 2004 Presidential Election
  - (1) Early exit polls reported strong support for Democrat
  - (2) Republican won
  - (3) Polls seemed totally unreliable
- e. Focus Group Research
  - (1) Very valuable
- f. Midterm Elections: 2006
- g. Election of 2008
  - (1) Election of first African-American President
  - (2) "New Hampshire Debacle"
3. Initiatives and referenda
  - a. Types of "elections" in which voters are asked opinions on specific issues
  - b. If question specific enough and worded correctly, could be valid measures
4. Interest groups and "grass-roots" contact
  - a. Also unscientific
  - b. Interest-group leaders' opinions may not reflect members' opinions on many issues
  - c. Most people never express opinions unless they are heavily involved in issue
5. Mass media
  - a. Can also be unreliable
  - b. Measurement of time spent or space devoted "for" or "against" an issue
  - c. Most letters to editors of newspapers negative
  - d. Most people do not write letters to editors of newspapers
  - e. Public does not always adopt opinion put forth by media
E. Intensity and stability of public opinion
  1. Intensity refers to how strongly someone feels about an issue
  2. Stability refers to how long public has held certain opinion on issue
  3. *Popular opinion* not same as *public opinion*
     - a. Public opinion usually well thought out
     - b. Popular opinion response to significant news item often without knowing the "facts"
  4. Influences on intensity and stability of public opinion
     - a. Same factors that influence the content influence intensity and stability
     - b. Political efficacy

14th Edition

(1) Refers to person's feeling of political power
(2) The more politically efficacious person feels, the more intense the opinion usually

F. When is a poll not a poll?
(1) Dishonest pollsters
(2) Push polls
   a. Attempts to change opinions of respondents
   b. Used late in an election campaign

III. The Future
A. Public may demand more correspondence between public opinion and public policy
B. Public may just "drop out" and leave governing to "experts"

Important Terms

Political socialization	Formal elites	Direct socialization
Indirect socialization	Public opinion	Peers
Mass media	Latent opinions	Socio-economic background
Stability of opinion	Opinion leaders	Informal elites
Gallup and Roper	Popular opinion	Intensity of opinion
Tiananmen Square	Eric Honiker	Margin of Error
Political efficacy	Public opinion poll	Referenda
Initiatives	Filter effect	Exit polls
Push polls	Forced opinion	Focus group
Bradley Effect	Roper and Gallup	

Multiple Choice Questions

Circle the number of the correct answer.

1. Normally, the most important source of political socialization is the

(1) family
(2) schools
(3) peers
(4) television
(5) co-workers.

14th Edition

2. What may become the main source of political socialization when parents are frequently absent when children are home?

   (1) schools
   (2) peers
   (3) clergy
   (4) books
   (5) rock music.

3. Probably the second major source of political socialization is

   (1) peers
   (2) the family
   (3) clergy
   (4) television
   (5) schools.

4. Opinions that are not expressed are called

   (1) militant opinions
   (2) submerged opinions
   (3) lithe opinions
   (4) latent opinions
   (5) obscured opinions.

5. The developers of the first scientific public opinion polls were

   (1) Roper and Gallup
   (2) Harris and Gallup
   (3) Harris and Roper
   (4) Harris, Gallup and Roper
   (5) The University of Michigan Public Opinion Research Center.

6. When a public opinion poll measures how strong someone's opinion about a particular question is, the poll is measuring a characteristic called

   (1) political efficacy
   (2) saliency
   (3) intensity
   (4) latency
   (5) obfuscation.

7. When a public opinion poll measures how much a person thinks his/her opinion really matters to anyone else, the poll is measuring a characteristic called

    (1) intensity
    (2) political efficacy
    (3) saliency
    (4) latency
    (5) obfuscation.

8. Traditional thinking regarding public opinion asserts that

    (1) public opinion is nice to know but relatively unimportant to the behavior of the government
    (2) elites really are the ones who formulate public opinion among the masses
    (3) elite opinion is important, not the opinion of the masses
    (4) public opinion is only important in a democracy
    (5) public opinion is the driving force behind the behavior of the government in a democracy.

9. The elitist view of public opinion asserts that

    (1) public opinion is nice to know but relatively unimportant to the behavior of the government
    (2) elite opinion is important, not the opinion of common people
    (3) elites really are the ones who formulate mass public opinion
    (4) public opinion is the driving force behind the behavior of the government in a democracy
    (5) public opinion is only important in a democracy.

10. Who would be most likely to be an opinion leader to a United States Supreme Court justice? (Think about this one; it's not in the book.)

    (1) lobbyists
    (2) the justice's law clerk (just graduated from law school)
    (3) a syndicated newspaper columnist
    (4) a Harvard Law School professor who writes about the law in journals that justices read
    (5) his/her spouse.

11. When people create an opinion, when asked, even if they had not really thought about the issue before, the resulting opinion is referred to as a(n)

   (1) forced opinion
   (2) projected opinion
   (3) latent opinion
   (4) pulled opinion
   (5) contradictory opinion

Fill-in-the-Blank Questions

Write the appropriate word or words in the blanks provided.

1. The process by which we acquire our political attitudes is called

   _____ .

2. Differences in political behavior are often the result of differences in political _____ . (Be specific)

3. _____ is the process by which attitudes and ideas are deliberately taught.

4. _____ occurs when someone learns behavior by observing others.

5. The five sources of political socialization are

   (1) _____
   (2) _____
   (3) _____
   (4) _____
   (5) _____ .

6. _____ consists of beliefs shared by a relatively large group of people on matters of public concern.

7. People who have a more than normal sway on what other people think are called _____ .

8. _____ and _____ are kinds of elections where the voters are asked their opinions on specific issues.

9. Besides measuring the content of public opinion, pollsters might also want to measure the _____ and the _____ of public opinion.

94

Chapter 7

10. A person's feeling regarding his/her own political power is called _____.

11. _____ is a "knee jerk" reaction often to a significant news story of the day and frequently without the respondent knowing the "facts."

12. The major incident in China that demonstrated that the Chinese government was willing to use deadly force to maintain it authoritarian control occurred in Beijing in a place known as _____.

13. The former East German dictator who was forced from office largely as because of massive, negative public opinion was _____.

14. A(n) _____ poll is one in which the pollster is actually trying to influence the respondent to support a particular presidential candidate, for example.

15. Polls taken among voters as they leave the polling places during an election cause problems in predicting close presidential elections. These polls are called _____ .

16. A polling phenomenon that may or may not exist, called the _____, occurs when those being polled lie about their support for a minority-race candidate for fear of being labeled racist.

17. Radio, television, and the Internet are all examples of a means of transmitting information called the _____ .

18. Researchers use _____ to understand why people think the way they do about a certain issue or candidate, rather than what they think.

19. People who can influence the opinions of government office holders are called _____ elites.

True/False Questions

Write the correct answer in the blanks provided.

1. When a teacher tells a first-grade students that they must be attentive when other students are speaking, the teacher is utilizing direct socialization. _____

2. When the teachers themselves are not attentive to students when they talk, they may produce indirect socialization. _____

3. The sources of political socialization have not changed in the last 100 years in the United States. _____

4. Schools tend to teach American children to be "free thinkers" and not to support the governmental system without a great deal of critical thinking. _____

5. Organizations such as the Girl Scouts are merely social organizations and, therefore, perform no role in the political socialization process. _____

6. A large majority of the adult population get most of their political information from television; therefore, television is the most important source of political socialization. _____

7. Suppose we asked 5000 Americans, selected in a random sample, their opinions on military spending. When we tabulated the results, we would then have public opinion data. _____

8. Today members of the clergy are the most important source of our public opinions. _____

9. Since people like Oprah Winfrey and the Sean Penn are merely entertainers, people do not pay attention to their political opinions. _____

10. Studies have shown that television can make people think whatever television wants them to think without much difficulty. _____

11. The "filter effect" refers to a mental process by which people hear and see only what they want to hear and see, so to speak. _____

12. What matters in a public opinion poll is what people think about a given subject right now. What they thought about it last week, last year, or ten years ago is not important. _____

13. Public opinion polls will always have a margin of error.

Discussion Questions

Use your own paper to answer the following questions.

1. All of us have experienced direct and indirect socialization. Give one example of each from your own experience, and explain why your example is direct or indirect socialization.

2. What are the sources of political socialization. Explain the role of each.

3. Although they came from essentially the same sources, how do political socialization and public opinion differ from each other?

4. Why might a latent opinion become a public opinion?

5. Define an opinion leader. Give an example of a person who is an opinion leader to you and tell why you consider him/her to be an opinion leader for you.

Using Your Little Grey Cells

1. Go to the library reference section where you will find Gallup polls, *New York Times*/CBS polls, or other public opinion polls. Write a brief report about public opinion over the past 15 years concerning any issue that interests you. (You might also want to know something about the people who responded to your poll; for example, how old they are, what their family income is, their race, religion, sex, etc.

2. Instead of going to the library to find complete public opinion data, go to The Gallup Organization's web site at http://www.gallup.com/. Find some recent data on some controversial issue such as gun control or abortion. Explain what Gallup polls reveal about this issue. Also, at this web site, find how Gallup conducts its polls.

PARTICIPATION

THE KEY TO
DEMOCRATIC GOVERNMENT

CHAPTER 8
VOTER BEHAVIOR

Learning Objectives

After reading and studying the chapter on voter behavior in the text, you should have a better understanding of the following:

1. Why people should vote;
2. The qualifications for voting;
3. Why some people cannot vote and why some just do not vote;
4. How changing voter qualifications might increase voter turnout;
5. The factors that influence individual and group voter behavior.

Chapter Outline

I. Qualifications for Voting
   A. Citizenship
      1. Native-born or naturalized
      2. Not all countries require citizenship for voting
      3. Not required in all states at one time in United States
   B. Registration
      1. Only required since late in 19th century
      2. Required in all states except North Dakota
         a. Residency on day of registration in about 60% the states
         b. Residency of 10-30 days before registration in remainder
      4. Types of registration
         a. Permanent
            (1) Once registered always registered
            (2) Exception: person moves or dies!
         b. Periodic
            (1) Everyone must reregister every ten years
            (2) Expensive and time-consuming
   C. Residency
      1. Must live in state and district voter wishes to vote in for period of time before voting
      2. Required because of
         a. Voter fraud
         b. Need for familiarity with local issues
      3. Civil Rights Act of 1970 allows no more than 30-days' residency for presidential elections

4. Supreme Court declared lengthy residency requirements for state and local elections unconstitutional
 D. Age
   1. Eighteen years old
   2. Made uniform throughout states by 26th Amendment

II. Who Cannot Vote
 A. Those not registered, not citizens, not at least 18
 B. Prisoners
 C. Mental incompetents (legally declared so)
 D. Convicted felons
 E. Those convicted of voter fraud
 F. Citizens living outside United States
   1. Exception: military personnel
   2. Those outside country may obtain absentee ballots where allowed

III. Nonvoting
 A. Most people eligible to vote don't vote
 B. Presidential elections get most voters
 C. Reasons for nonvoting
   1. Legal reasons
     a. Noncompulsory voting laws
       (1) Many countries impose penalties for not voting
       (2) Voter turnout increases with compulsory voting laws
     b. Registration
       (1) Can be a "hassle"
       (2) Trend toward easier registration
         • Federal law now requires states to allow registration when renewing driver's license, by mail, when applying for public assistance
     c. Number of elections in one year
       (1) European countries usually have no more than one election per year
       (2) Some states may have numerous elections per year
       (3) Turnout lowest in "off-year" elections
     d. Absentee ballots
       (1) All states allow some absentee balloting
       (2) Process in some states is a hassle
       (3) Significant increases in absentee balloting
       (4) Increased voter fraud
   2. Lack of party organization and competition

14th edition

a. Parties not highly organized
b. Parties not highly differentiated
c. Largest percentage of nonvoting occurs in lower classes
d. Produces voter apathy
e. Formal education level most powerful predictor of voter behavior

IV. Determinants of Voter Choice
   A. Candidates
      1. Image
         a. Integrity
         b. Reliability
         c. Competence
      2. Voters' perception of how well candidate can do job
      3. Voter prejudices
   B. Party affiliation
      1. Less important today but still significant
      2. Fastest growing group of voters: independents
      3. "Independents" not really that independent
   C. Ideology
      1. Closely related to party affiliation
      2. Neither party strongly ideological
      3. However, voter perception may be that they are ideological
   D. Issues
      1. Least important factor in voter choice
      2. Difficult to separate from other three, however
      3. Economic issues do seem to have the most relevance
      4. Hard issues/soft issues

V. Voting Patterns
   A. Sex
      1. Women tend to vote Democrat
      2. Women perceive Democrat party as champions of poor and minorities
   B. Race, national origin, and religion
      1. Blacks, Hispanics generally, Eastern Europeans, and Irish tend to vote Democrat
      2. Catholics and Jews tend to vote Democrat
      3. Cubans tend to vote Republican
   C. Social and economic class and occupation
      1. Lower social and economic classes tend to vote Democrat
      2. Upper social and economic classes and highly educated tend to vote Republican

Chapter 8

14th edition

3. Blue-collar workers tend to vote Democrat
4. Professionals tend to vote Republican with some notable exceptions
D. Age
1. Younger voters tend not to vote generally
2. Democrat identification strongest among those under 30 and over 50
E. Place of residence
1. Big-city residents tend to vote Democrat
2. Small-city and urban residents tend to vote Republican
3. Midwest has highest percentage of independent voters
4. East has strongest identification with Democrats
5. South votes more Democratic except for president
6. Far West has fairly even split among Democrats, Republicans, and independents
F. Does Your Vote Really Matter?

Important Terms

Permanent registration
Periodic registration
Absentee ballot
Enfranchisement
Ideology
Demographic characteristics
"Easy" issues
Twenty-sixth Amendment
"Off-year" election
Purging

Absentee ballot
Residency
Noncompulsory voting laws
Voter apathy
Party affiliation
"Hard" issues
Voter turnout
"Voting the graveyard"
"Echo chamber effect"

Multiple Choice Questions

Circle the number of the correct answer.

1. The constitutional amendment that lowered the voting age to 18 in all states was the

   (1) 22nd Amendment
   (2) 23rd Amendment
   (3) 24th Amendment
   (4) 25th Amendment
   (5) 26th Amendment.

2. Only one state does not require registration of voters, namely the state of

   (1) Montana
   (2) North Dakota
   (3) South Dakota
   (4) Massachusetts
   (5) Illinois.

3. The Civil Rights Act of 1970 does not permit residency requirements for presidential elections of more than

   (1) 100 days
   (2) 30 days
   (3) 50 days
   (4) 60 days
   (5) 90 days.

4. Which one of the following is apparently the least important determinant of voter behavior?

   (1) Issues
   (2) Candidates' personal characteristics
   (3) Voter's perception of candidates' ability to do the job
   (4) Ideology
   (5) Candidate's party affiliation.

14th edition

5. In considering "issues" as a determinant of voter behavior, one issue seems to be consistently quite important to voters, namely the issue of

(1) capital punishment
(2) abortion
(3) military spending
(4) the crime rate
(5) economics.

6. In the United States, most people eligible to vote usually
(1) cast their votes consistently for Democrat candidates
(2) cast their votes consistently for Republican candidates
(3) cast their votes for independent candidates
(4) cast their votes for a mixture of all three types of candidates
(5) do not vote at all.

7. Purging, in the political sense, refers to

(1) what the Romans used to do after they ate too much
(2) refusing to allow felons and mental incompetents to vote
(3) not counting absentee ballots when voter fraud is suspected
(4) removing the names of people who have moved or died from the voter lists.

8. The two major parties in the United States supposedly direct their policies and programs to the _____ voters.

(1) upper class
(2) middle class
(3) lower class
(4) the poorest
(5) Christian and Jewish

8. Candidates for political office in the United States often

(1) do *not* take clear-cut stands on controversial issues
(2) take clear-cut stands on controversial issues
(3) do *not* try to appeal to most voters
(4) do try to appeal to most voters
(5) both #1 and #4.

Fill-in-the-Blank Questions

Write the appropriate word or words in the blanks provided.

1. In most states, the four qualifications for voting are

   (1) _____
   (2) _____
   (3) _____
   (4) _____ .

2. _____ registration means that once a person registers to vote, he/she remains on the list of eligible voters until that person moves or dies.

3. Some states require _____ registration in which all persons must register to vote again every decade.

4. Persons who are not physically able to vote on election day may obtain _____ ballots so that they may participate in the election.

5. The economic class of people who tend to vote least is the _____ class.

6. Many states exclude a number of persons from voting for reasons other than age, citizenship, registration, or residency. List four of these groups of people who are often prohibited from voting.

   (1) _____
   (2) _____
   (3) _____
   (4) _____

7. In referring to elections, the term _____ means the election was not held in the same year as a presidential election.

8. The condition in which the voter believes that his/her vote doesn't really matter and that things will remain pretty much the same whether he/she votes or not is called voter _____ .

9. Surveys conducted in 2008 indicate that a slight majority voters self-identified as members of the _____ Party or at least leaning in that direction.

14th edition

10. When candidates for the same public office take identical positions on issues or take no position at all on the same issues, then the voters are said to be experiencing the _____.

11. The term used to denote the number of potential voters who actually voted, usually expressed as a percentage, is called voter _____ .

12. The term used to describe population characteristics such as age, race, sex, place of residence, etc., is _____ characteristics.

13. The one characteristic that is the greatest predictor of voter behavior is the person's _____.

14. Give an example of some current issue in American politics that would be considered a "soft" issue. _____

True/False Questions

Write the correct answer in the blanks provided.

1. To vote in the United States, a person must have been born in the United States. _____

2. Not all countries have citizenship requirements for voting. ____

3. Requiring registration as a qualification for voting was primarily a result of voter fraud. _____

4. Residency requirements for voting today vary from 1 day to 2 years from state to state. _____

5. Because Americans take voting very seriously, the United States has one of the highest voter turnouts among democratic countries. _____

6. Voter turnout in the United States today is greater than it has ever been before. _____

7. Absentee ballots have never changed the outcome of an election in the United States. _____

14th edition

8. Anyone, 18 years of age or older, who is a citizen and who is registered to vote, is required to vote in most states in the United States. _____

9. The poor have the greatest record of voter turnout in the United States because they get more services from the government than other groups do. _____

10. People tend to vote in greater numbers in presidential-election years than in "off-year" elections. _____

11. People with higher incomes tend to vote more frequently than people with lower incomes. _____

12. Since most states have made voting easier, voter fraud is declining. _____

13. Wealthier, more-educated people are more likely to vote Republican. _____

14. Cuban Americans, unlike other Hispanics, tend to vote Republican because Republicans are perceived to be more opposed to the current Cuban government. _____

15. In recent decades, it has become clear that voters are not willing to split their ticket when voting. _____

16. The United States is the only country in recent times to have lower voter turnout than would be expected in a democracy. _____

17. The younger the voters, the more likely they are to vote for Democrat candidates. _____

18. Independent candidates get their most support from potential voters early in an election year. _____

Discussion Questions

Use your own paper to answer the following questions.

1. Define the term *democracy*. Based on what you know about voter behavior, is the United States a democracy? Explain.

Chapter 8

14th edition

2. Define the term *voter apathy*. What would you do to decrease this phenomenon among American voters?

3. Why do things other than issues seem more important in determining voter choices at the polls?

4. What is the "echo chamber effect?" How does it relate to voter behavior?

5. Differentiate between "hard" and "easy" issues. How do they relate to voter behavior? Give examples of each.

Using Your Little Gray Cells

1. Find out the demographic characteristics of the people who live in your local area; for example, religion, race, income, occupation, national origin, etc. Find out what issue or issues seem to be important in your area. Then, using the information you have concerning voter behavior in general, write a brief essay outlining the campaign strategy you would use if you were seeking the office of mayor or city councilperson, for example. (Hint: local demographic information can often be obtained from the local Chamber of Commerce; information about issues can, of course, be found in local newspapers or television news broadcasts.)

2. Answer the following about voter registration in your state:

   (1) Where does one go to register to vote?
   (2) What residency requirements are there?
   (3) Can college students who are not permanent residents of the college area register to vote in the area in which they attend college?
   (4) Does your state have permanent or periodic registration?
   (5) How far in advance of an election must a person register if he/she wishes to vote in that election?

Chapter 8

14th edition

Chapter 9

Campaigns and Elections

Learning Objectives

After reading and studying the chapter on campaigns and elections in the text, you should have a better understanding of the following:

1. The kinds of elections held in the United States and how they are conducted;
2. What offices are elected at the national, state, and local levels;
3. The Electoral College;
4. The elements of a successful campaign;
5. How campaign money is spent;
6. The regulation of campaign spending and why it is regulated;
7. How successful regulation of campaign spending has been.

Chapter Outline

I. How Elections Are Conducted
  A. How America votes
    1. Voting technology
      a. Punch cards
        • Being replaced by electronic voting
        • States given money via the Help America Vote Act
      b. Optical scanners
      c. Voting machines
      d. Paper ballots
      e. Electronic voting (Direct Recording Electronic voting)
    2. Ballot design
      a. Electronic ballot with a paper trail
      b. Butterfly ballot
    3. Early voting and absentee balloting
  B. Types of elections
    1. Party primaries
      a. Select the parties' nominees
      b. Held weeks or months in advance of the general election
      c. For party members only
    2. General elections
      a. Choose the persons to actually hold office from among nominees of parties and independents
      b. Independents are candidates without party affiliation
    3. Types of party primaries (sometimes just called *primaries*)
      a. Closed
      b. Only registered party members may participate
      c. Examples
        • New York
        • Pennsylvania

110
Chapter 9

- Florida
  - d. Semi-closed
    - (1) Independents can vote in one or the other party's primaries (not both)
    - (2) Examples
      - Oregon
      - New Jersey
      - Massachusetts
  - e. Open
    - (1) No party preference required at registration
    - (2) Decision about which primary to vote in is made by the voter on primary-election day
    - (3) Examples
      - Most southern states
      - Ohio
      - Wisconsin
      - Michigan
      - Other states in upper Midwest
  - e. Blanket primary
    - (1) Variation of open primary
    - (2) All parties' candidates appear on same ballot
    - (3) Voter may choose only one candidate for each office
    - (4) Found only in Louisiana
  - f. Nonpartisan primary
  - g. Found most frequently in local elections
  - h. Candidates run as individuals, not party members
4. Voters prefer open primaries
5. Parties favor closed primaries
   - a. Closed primaries prevent crossover (raiding) voting
     - (1) Members of other party vote in opposing party's primary
     - (2) Difficult to do except in small geographic districts
6. Initiatives
   - a. Voters force government to do or not to do something
   - b. Comes from the voters to the voters on a ballot
   - c. Not found in all states
   - d. Cannot be used for national government at all
7. Referendums
   - a. Allow voters to show approval or disapproval of something government wants to do
   - b. Comes from legislative bodies to the voters on a ballot
   - c. Not found in all states
   - d. Cannot be used for national government at all
8. Recalls: allow voters to end official's term before it has expired

111

Chapter 9

D. Types of ballots
   1. Party column
      a. Lists candidates for all offices in columns by party
      b. Also called Indiana ballot
   2. Office group
      a. Lists candidates by office
      b. Also called Massachusetts ballot
   3. Straight-ticket voting
      a. Voting for all candidates of one party in general election
      b. Party-column ballot encourages straight-ticket voting
   4. Split-ticket voting: voting for candidates from more than one party or from party candidates and independents
E. Arrangement of names on ballot
   1. First name listed has advantage
   2. Some states list candidates at random instead of alphabetically
   3. Some states change first name on ballot in each voting district
F. Incumbent advantage
   1. Usually more well known
   2. Free publicity as a result of already holding office
   3. Frequently has more campaign experience
   4. Constituent services produce votes
   5. Has a record to stand on

II. Who Is Elected
A. President and vice president
   1. Only at-large election at national level
   2. Nomination
      a. By national party conventions
      b. Presidential primaries commit delegates to particular candidates at national conventions
      c. Therefore, nomination may actually be decided before the official nomination at the national convention
   3. Balancing the ticket may not be as important as it used to be.
   4. Election occurs on first Tuesday after first Monday in November every four years in even-numbered years
   5. Electoral College
      a. Constitutional framers considered people untrustworthy to elect president and vice president
      b. Each state's electoral vote equal to its congressional representation
      c. Electoral vote totals 538
      d. 270 needed to win
      e. Winner-take-all system generally
      f. Electors vote in early December

       g. If no one receives majority, House selects president and Senate selects vice president
    5. Electoral College reform
       a. Most popular proposal is do away with system altogether
       b. Why Electoral College remains
         (1) Traditional
         (2) Desire for change not constant
         (3) Large electoral-vote states reluctant to give up power
  B. Congress
    1. Directly elected
    2. In most states only a plurality of the vote required to elect
    3. When elections are held
       a. Every two years in even numbered years
       b. Entire House of Representatives
       c. Approximately 1/3 of the Senate
    4. Geographic regions
       a. Senators from entire state
       b. Representatives from districts within state
         (1) Reapportionment every 10 years
         (2) Average congressional district contains almost three-quarters of a million people
         (3) Gerrymandering
            • Rigging election district to favor one group over another
            • Charges of gerrymandering still occur on occasion
  C. State and local offices
    1. Organized similarly to national government
    2. More offices elected
    3. Time of election differs from state to state
       a. "Off-year" elections
       b. Voter turn out usually lower in off-years

III. Campaigns
  A. Elements of successful campaign
    1. "Marketable" candidate
       a. Intelligent, but still just plain folks
       b. Name recognition
       c. Optimistic
       d. Proper image
       e. Healthy
       f. Wants to win
    2. Effective Organization
       a. Candidate centered
       b. Finance committee
       c. Campaign consultants
       d. Campaign manager and staff

113

Chapter 9

e. Volunteers
3. Money
   a. Campaigns are expensive
   b. Sources of funding
      (1) Individual contributions
      (2) Political Action Committees
      (3) Political parties
      (3) Candidate's personal funds
      (4) Public financing
4. Federal campaign funding rules (and loopholes)
   a. Federal Elections Campaign Acts of 1971 and 1974
   b. Created Federal Election Commission
   c. Limited campaign contributions
   d. Loaded with loopholes
   e. Difficult to limit contributions because of Court interpretations of Constitution
   f. Independent expenditures
   g. Soft money
5. Changes in campaign financing
   a. Ban on the use of soft money at the national level
   b. Severely limits use of soft money at state level
   c. Prohibits interest groups from running issue ads 30 days prior to a primary and 60 days prior to a general election
   d. Doubles individual contributions to candidates per election to $2000
   e. Contribution limits raised extensively for candidates facing opponents who are self financed
   f. The impact of the Internet on fundraising
B. Where the money goes
   1. Campaign consultants
      a. Provide strategic planning and overall direction
      b. Necessary to successful campaign
   2. By type of expenditure
      a. Greatest amount spent on mass media, especially TV
      b. Direct mailing—targeting
C. Volunteers
   1. Save money for other expenses
   2. Effective advocates for candidate
D. The Internet
   1. Candidates and parties must maintain Web sites
      a. Raise money
      b. Secure volunteers
      c. Disperse information
   2. Blogs
IV. Conclusion

114

Chapter 9

14th Edition

A. Regulation decentralized
B. Media campaigning here to stay
C. Education of voter to offset "packaging" of candidates
D. Evil triumphs when good people do nothing

Important Terms

At-large elections
Independent expenditures
Independents
PAC
Off-year election
Straight-ticket voting
Party-column ballot
"Marketable" candidate
Balancing the ticket
Reapportionment
Nonpartisan primary
Federal Election
   Commission
Swing Districts
Bipartisan Campaign
   Reform Act, 2002

Primary elections
Closed primary
Crossover voting
Referendums
Office-group ballot
Split-ticket voting
Blanket primary
Constituents
Unpledged delegates
Campaign consultant
Pledged delegates
Twenty-Third
   Amendment
Butterfly ballot
Help America Vote Act
Electronic voting

Plurality
Issue ads
Recalls
Incumbent
Dark Horse
Soft money
Electoral College
General elections
Open primary
Gerrymandering
Initiatives
Federal Election
   Campaign Acts
Provisional ballots
527s
Majority

Multiple Choice Questions

Circle the number of the correct answer.

1. The total number of electoral votes in the Electoral College is

   (1) 270
   (2) 100
   (3) 435
   (4) 535
   (5) 538.

2. Elections in which the <u>winners</u> for various offices are selected by the voters from among party candidates and independents are called

   (1) party primaries
   (2) open primaries
   (3) closed primaries
   (4) general elections
   (5) initiatives.

3. Elections to <u>nominate</u> candidates for various offices are called

   (1) primaries
   (2) recall elections
   (3) referendums
   (4) general elections
   (5) initiatives.

4. A type of primary in which voters must register as party members before receiving that party's primary ballot is called a (an)

   (1) open primary
   (2) blanket primary
   (3) office-group primary
   (4) party column primary
   (5) closed primary.

5. A type of primary in which voters are not required to indicate a party preference before voting in the primary is called a (an)

   (1) open primary
   (2) general primary
   (3) office-group primary
   (4) party-column primary
   (5) closed primary.

6. A type of election used by voters to force government officials to do something the voters want or to prevent government from doing something the voters do not want is called a (an)

   (1) recall
   (2) purge
   (3) referendum
   (4) initiative
   (5) Nielson rating.

7. A type of election that allows voters to remove someone from office before his/her term expires is called a (an)

   (1) recall
   (2) purge
   (3) referendum
   (4) initiative
   (5) general election.

8. A type of election that allows voters to accept or reject certain measures that state legislatures or local governments pass is called a (an)

   (1) recall
   (2) purge
   (3) referendum
   (4) initiative
   (5) general election.

9. The president and the vice president are not elected directly by the people; rather, they are elected by the

   (1) Congress
   (2) Electoral College
   (3) House of Representatives
   (4) Senate
   (5) state legislatures

10. A type of primary where the candidates run as individuals and not as party members is called

   (1) an open primary
   (2) a nonpartisan primary
   (3) a closed primary
   (4) general primary
   (5) a blanket primary.

11. Only two states do not distribute their electoral votes by the winner-take-all system. Those two states are

   (1) Maine and Nebraska
   (2) New York and Louisiana
   (3) Montana and Michigan
   (4) Wisconsin and Illinois
   (5) California and Nebraska.

12. A type of primary in which independents can vote in one or the other party's primary is called a _____ primary.

   (1) semi-closed
   (2) semi-open
   (3) open
   (4) blanket
   (5) nonpartisan.

14th Edition

13. The greatest expenditure for any campaign for major offices is for

    (1) travel expenses
    (2) salaries of the campaign staff
    (3) direct mail
    (4) television advertising
    (5) public opinion polls.

14. Most states require a referendum for

    (1) raising property taxes
    (2) raising state income taxes
    (3) adding or doing away with the death penalty
    (4) constitutional amendments
    (5) changing the number of electors the state has.

15. When delegates to a national party convention go to the convention without committing their support to any candidate, the delegates are said to be _____.

    (1) demented
    (2) unpledged
    (3) pledged
    (4) scum bags
    (5) contrarians.

16. The District of Columbia acquired electoral votes through

    (1) an executive order
    (2) an act of Congress
    (3) a Supreme Court ruling
    (4) an amendment to the Constitution
    (5) custom.

17. The number of electoral votes required to be elected president is

    (1) 538
    (2) 100
    (3) 271
    (4) 270
    (5) 435

14th Edition

Fill-in-the-Blank Questions

Write the appropriate word or words in the blanks provided.

1. The power to conduct elections is reserved to the _____ government.

2. The _____ government must bear the cost of holding an election, even a presidential election.

3. A (An) _____ candidate is one who is not connected with any political party.

4. A (An) _____ is a person who already holds an office and is seeking re-election.

5. _____ voting means a person has voted for all candidates of one party.

6. _____ voting means a person has voted for some candidates of one party and some from another party or from independents.

7. The _____ ballot lists candidates under a party heading.

8. In a (an) _____ ballot, candidates are listed under the heading of the office they are seeking.

9. A variation on the open primary in which the voters can choose among the candidates from all the parties but in which voters are restricted to choosing only one candidate for each office is called a (an) _____ primary.

10. Presidential elections are held on the first _____ (day) after the first _____ (day) in _____ (month) every four years.

11. When vice-presidential candidates are selected because they possess some characteristics that are different from the presidential nominees, such as their religious preferences, the selection is said to be made in order to _____ .

12. Voters in a presidential election are actually casting votes for slates of _____ rather than for presidential and vice-presidential candidates.

13. Electors go to their respective state capitals to cast their ballots for president and for vice president early in the month of _____ .

14. If no candidates receive a majority of the vote in the Electoral College, the _____ selects the president and the _____ selects the vice president.

15. The distribution of seats in the House of Representatives after the census every ten years is called _____ .

16. Drawing election district boundaries to favor one group or party over another is called _____ .

17. The state _____ is responsible for reapportioning the voting districts every ten years.

18. If election districts are drawn illegally, the _____ will re-draw the district lines.

19. The three elements of a successful campaign are

    (1) _____
    (2) _____
    (3) _____

20. The so-called _____ ballot caused major problems in the 2004 presidential election in the state of Florida.

21. The _____ was created to regulate campaign financing for candidates for national office.

22. The _____ , a relatively new technology, has proved to be a viable means of raising campaign funds and for recruiting volunteers.

23. When a candidate is elected by getting one more vote than any other candidate, but not a majority, then that candidate is said to have been elected by a _____ of the vote.

24. The people who live in a representative's district or a senator's state, for example, are referred to as their _____ , i.e., the people they represent.

25. No state can have fewer than _____ electoral votes.

26. A _____ presidential candidate is one who is not widely known but who manages to get a party's nomination for the office.

27. Election districts where there would be strong campaigns from both the major political parties, resulting in either one's having a good chance of winning the district are called _____ districts.

28. The main components of the Bispartisan Campaign Reform Act of 2002 are

   (1) _____

   (2) _____

   (3) _____

   (4) _____

29. Money is funneled to candidates by means of _____ , which allow independent expenditures in unlimited amounts as long as the candidates or their campaigns have no say in how the money is spent.

30. When a person comes to vote whose name is not found among the eligible voters, the individual is given a _____, which is sealed and kept until the potential voter's status is clarified.

True/False Questions

Write the correct answer in the blanks provided.

1. "Raiding" cannot occur very readily in states with closed primaries. _____

2. Initiatives and referendums can be used at all levels of government: national, state, and local. _____

3. The arrangement of names on a ballot has no bearing on the outcome of an election. _____

4. Only U. S. Senators and U. S. Representatives are elected at large. _____

5. In each state during a presidential election, electors must receive a majority of the votes to be elected. _____

6. In most states, the Electoral College. electors can vote for candidates they did not represent on the ballot. _____

7. All presidents have been elected by the Electoral College. _____

8. In most states, a majority of the popular vote is required to elect members of Congress. _____

14th Edition

9. Since voting procedures had become more sophisticated as time passed and people had become used to voting, gerrymandering has not been a problem since the early 1800s. _____

10. There are more officials elected at the national level than at the state and levels because the national government is much larger than any state. _____

11. Voter turnout for state elections is always larger during an "off-year" than it is during a presidential election year. _____

12. Wealthy presidential candidates have an advantage because they have tremendous amounts of their own money to spend on their campaigns *besides federal matching funds*. _____

13. Most Americans contribute money to political campaigns. _____

14. In the general election for president, if a candidate accepts public funding, there is a limit on the amount of the candidate's personal money that he/she can spend. _____

15. Voting technology has not changed much in the last fifty years since most states still use paper ballots. _____

16. A small number of states could actually decide who the president and the vice president will be. _____

17. One of the main differences between a referendum and an initiative is that the referendum comes to the voters from some legislative body, whereas the initiative comes from the voters to the voters on a ballot.

18. Provisional ballots are those that are put aside because a voter has said that the candidate he/she voted for was not the candidate that the voting machine counted. _____

19. An election in California for a United States Senate seat would be an at-large election. _____

20. Because the District of Columbia is not a state, it has no electoral votes. _____

Discussion Questions

Use your own paper to answer the following questions.

1. Why is it difficult to defeat an incumbent in an election?

2. Why did the writers of the Constitution choose to have the president and the vice president elected by the Electoral College?

3. Compose an argument in favor of or against retaining the Electoral College?

4. From what sources do presidential candidates get campaign funds? Why do they need so much money? Should we continue funding campaigns in this way or not? Explain. If not, how should they be funded? What political consequences might accrue if the changes you suggest were implemented?

5. Explain why it is difficult to control campaign spending.

Using Your Little Gray Cells

1. Using newspaper and magazine articles, *Who's Who* and your own knowledge, decide which of the two presidential candidates in the 2008 election was more "marketable." Explain your choice.

2. Assume you wanted to run for a policy-making position in local government (e.g., mayor, city council, commissioner, etc.). Design a campaign explaining what you would need to do, how much money you would have to raise, how you would raise these funds, what kind of help would you need, etc.

3. Interview a candidate for political office. Find out what a typical day of campaigning is like and report your findings to the class.

4. As indicated in this chapter, there are literally thousands of political action committees in the United States. Not all of them are well known like the PACs for big business segments and labor unions. Here is a list of a few of the more "exotic" PACs. Pick one, go to the Internet and see what you can find out about your choice.

- ItchPAC
- Extraterrestrial Phenomena PAC
- PawPAC
- Coca Cola Enterprises PAC
- HoofPac

123
Chapter 9

14th Edition

Chapter 10

Congress
The People's Branch

Learning Objectives

After reading and studying the chapter on Congress in the text, you sho better understanding of the following:

1. The institutional context of Congress;
2. The functions and responsibilities of Congress;
3. Constitutional requirements for membership in the House and Senate;
4. The demographic characteristics of members of Congress;
5. Political organization of Congress
6. Congressional tenure of office;
7. How a law is made;
8. Congressional committee system
9. Congressional voting behavior;
10. Leadership within the Congress.

Chapter Outline

I. The Institutional Context of Congress
   A. A "congress" is a two-year election cycle
   B. A "congress divided into sessions
   C. Representation
      1. Representing individuals
      2. Representing interest groups
   3. Representing districts or states
   D. Pork barrel legislation
      • Designed to promote re-election
   E. Voting on legislation
      1. Personal knowledge
      2. District majority
      3. Advice from associates
      4. Party loyalty
   F. Structure
      1. Bicameral
      2. Each state has 2 Senators
      3. House membership based on population of the state relative to other states
      4. House size fixed by law in 1911 at 435
      5. House reapportioned after census
   G. Tenure of Office
      1. Average number of terms for House members = 5 terms
      2. Average number of terms for Senate members = 2 terms
      3. Workload, expertise, and specialization required of members of Congress contributes to "professional politician" phenomenon

125

Chapter 10

II. Functions and Responsibilities
    A. The power of the purse
    B. Lawmaking
    C. Oversight
    D. Necessary to maintain balance between executive and Congress
    E. Determines if laws are being properly carried out
    F. Public education
        1. Speaking to local groups
        2. Writing articles for local newspapers
        3. Communicating with constituents by direct mail
    G. Conflict resolution
        1. United States a pluralistic society--many different interests
        2. Compromises often necessary
    H. Constituent services (Casework)
        1. Help for the individual with problems with the federal government
        2. District or state-wide benefits
        3. Obtaining federal money for projects within state or district
        4. Also referred to as casework

III. Political Organization of Congress
    A. Party organization
        1. Majority party controls each house
            a. Agenda
            b. Committees
                (1) Standing Committees
                (2) Appropriations Committee
    B. House and Senate quite different institutionally
        1. Little cooperation between parties in House
        2. Much more in the Senate
        3. Political leadership in House
            a. Speaker of the House
            b. Majority leader
            c. Minority leader
            d. Majority whips
            e. Minority whips
        4. Political leadership in Senate
            a. Vice president votes in case of a tie
            b. President pro-tempore
            c. Majority leader equivalent to Speaker of House Minority leader
            d. Whips
    C. Congressional committee system
        1. Congress organized into committees
        2. Most work takes place within committees
        3. Subcommittees
        4. Extremely important in House

5. Less so in Senate
6. Rules
   a. Rules for entire House or Senate
   b. Rules for a particular full committee of the House or Senate
   c. Rules for a particular sub-committee of the House or Senate
7. Types of committees
   a. Standing
   b. Select
   c. Joint

D. Committee staff
  1. Employees of Congress who work for a committee
  2. Not the same as a member's personal or legislative staffs
  3. Patronage appointments

E. Options when considering legislation
  1. Report legislation out favorably
  2. Report legislation out unfavorably
  3. Refuse to consider legislation

IV. Passing a Law
  A. Bills originate from a variety of sources
  B. Must have elected member of Congress to sponsor (introduce) it
  C. Introducing a bill
  D. Revenue bills (tax bills) must originate in the House
  E. Appropriations bills by custom originate in the House
  F. Each bill has sponsor(s)
    1. House
      a. Bill placed in hopper
      b. Numbered: HR designates a House bill
      c. Printed
      d. Distributed
    2 Senate
      a. Introduced by Senator
      b. Numbered: S designates a Senate bill
      c. Printed
      d. Distributed
    3. Types of bills
      a. Resolutions: concern internal business of either chamber or reflect sentiment of both House and Senate on some subject
      b. Private bills: pertain only to individuals named in bill
      c. Public bills: generally apply to everyone
    4. Assignment to committee
      a. House: Speaker of the House assigns bills to committees
      b. Senate: presiding officer assigns bills to committees
  D. In committee
    1. Study bills and make recommendations to chamber
    2. Divided into subcommittees
      a. Hold hearings if they like the bill

127

Chapter 10

b. Report bill to full committee
3. Full committee action
   a. Could hold hearings itself
   b Report bill out as it came from subcommittee
   c. Amend bill and report it out as amended
   d. Vote to "kill" bill
   e. Report bill out to chamber with unfavorable recommendation
   f. If bill not reported out, chamber may invoke discharge petition (in House) or special resolution (in Senate)

E. Committee chairpersons
1. Powerful enough to "kill" a bill in committee
2. Call committee meetings
3. Establish agendas
4. Hire and fire committee staff
5. Arrange and chair hearings and markups
6. Designate conferees
7. Act as floor managers
8. Control committee funds and rooms
9. Regulate internal affairs and organization of committees

F. House passage
1. Bill placed on calendar
   a. Union Calendar: bills dealing with raising or spending money
   b. House Calendar: all other major public bills
   c. Private Calendar: private bills
   d. Consent Calendar: non-controversial bills
   e. Discharge Calendar: bills from discharge petition
2. Rules Committee
   a. Schedules bills for consideration in order of importance
   b. Organizes debate by establishing rules
   c. Very powerful committee which can kill a bill
3. Floor action
   a. Committee of Whole
   b. Amendments
     • Open rule
     • Closed rule
4. Voting: simple majority needed to pass

G. Senate passage
1. Bill placed on calendar
   a. Calendar of General Orders: all public and private bills
   b. Executive Calendar: all treaties and nominations
2. Floor action
   a. Unanimous consent: Parties agree in advance to the rules and time for bill's debate
   b. Motion
     (1) Usually controversial bills
     (2) Filibuster could occur

                    (a) Unlimited debate
                    (b) Goal: to kill bill
                    (c) Cloture
                        (1) Filibuster ended by about 3/5 majority vote
                        (2) Cloture vote seldom successful
            c.   Voting: simple majority needed for passage
    H.   Conference Committee
        1.   Irons out differences between versions of bill
        2.   Usually 3 to 7 members from each chamber
        3.   Generally drawn from the committees in each chamber who dealt
             with the bill originally
        4.   Speaker appoints House members
        5.   Presiding officer of Senate appoints Senate members
        6.   Bill sent back to each chamber in identical form for vote
    I.   Executive consideration
        1.   Sign bill into law
        2.   Not sign it
            a.   Becomes law without signature within 10 working
                 days if Congress still in session
            b.   Dies if Congress not in session within 10 working days
                 (Pocket Veto)
        3.   Veto it
            a.   Lists objections and returns bill to Congress
            b.   Congressional override by 2/3 majority of both chambers
            c.   No presidential item veto power
V.   Conclusion

    A.   Members of Congress are politicians
    B.   Use the technical process of lawmaking to for political ends
        1.   Redistribute wealth
        2.   Redistribute prestige
        3.   Redistribute security
        4.   Members usually put together alliances of votes for enacting laws
             that reflect the particular interests of state, district, or interest groups.
        5.   Lest we forget: the United States is organized into states, districts,
             and interest groups.

Important Terms

.cralism
.n Amendment
16th Amendment
Constituent service
Discharge petition
Union Calendar
Private legislation
House Calendar
Discharge Calendar
Sunshine rules
Rules Committee
Standing committee
12th Amendment
Majority floor leader
Speaker of the House
Mark up a bill
Rider amendment

Unanimous consent
Pork barrel legislation
Congressional Record
President Pro Tempore
Seniority system
"Professional politician"
Ways and Means Committee
Private Calendar
Conference committee
Executive session
Consent Calendar
Executive Calendar
Calendar of General Orders
Minority floor leader
Appropriations Committee
Committee of the Whole
Power of the purse

Article I
Oversight
Resolutions
Hopper
Public bills
Filibuster
Item veto
Cloture
Pocket veto
Open rule
Closed rule
Majority whip
Minority whip
Five-minute rule
Motion
Special resolution
Authorization bills

Multiple Choice Questions

Circle the number of the correct answer.

1. The 16th Amendment allowed

    1) Senators to be elected by state legislatures
    2) Senators to be elected by the voters
    3) Congress to pass income-tax laws
    4) The president the power of an item veto
    5) Congress the power to choose the president if no one receives a majority of the electoral vote.

2. The 20th Amendment allows

    1) Congress the power to pass resolutions
    2) Senators to be elected by the voters
    3) Congress to pass income-tax laws
    4) Congress the power to decide who will be acting president in case of emergency
    5) Congress the power to pass private legislation

3. A Congressional committee that is permanent is called

    1) A standing committee
    2) An executive committee
    3) A conference committee
    4) A joint committee
    5) A committee of the whole

4. When a committee finalizes a bill, it is said to have _____ the bill.

    1) Bought
    2) Accepted
    3) Marked up
    4) Beat up
    5) Clotured

5. Membership in the House has been fixed by law at

    1) 250 members
    2) 535 members
    3) 538 members
    4) 435 members
    5) 438 members.

6. The committee that controls the flow of legislation in the House is the

    1) Controller Committee
    2) Wretched Committee
    3) Permanent Committee
    4) Rules Committee
    5) Select Committee

7. In the House, when bills are introduced they are placed in the

    1) Toilet
    2) Hopper
    3) Bin
    4) Calendar
    5) Mark up

8. When members of Congress help the residents of their districts/states with problems they may be having with the federal government, the legislators are performing

   1) constituent service
   2) caseload
   3) oversight
   4) public education
   5) conflict resolution.

9. When Congress reviews how legislation already passed is being implemented, the Congress is performing its function of

   1) public education
   2) federal service
   3) oversight
   4) casework
   5) conflict resolution.

10. When members of Congress provide information to help citizens understand governmental action, the Congress is performing its function of

    1) casework
    2) federal service
    3) oversight
    4) public education
    5) conflict resolution.

11. Since Congress represents constituents with varying and often opposing viewpoints, there is a great deal of compromising that goes on. This process of compromise is often referred to as the congressional function of

    1) casework
    2) federal service
    3) oversight
    4) conflict resolution
    5) public education.

14th Edition

12. The evolutionary changes in Congress over the years that require members to be specialists have produced

   1) The filibuster tactic in the Senate
   2) Professional politicians
   3) The House Rules Committee
   4) Open rules
   5) Standing committees.

13. The House committee that would be assigned a bill to increase the federal tax on cigarettes would be

   1) Appropriations Committee
   2) Federal Tax Committee
   3) Ways and Means
   4) Select Committee
   5) Conference Committee

14. When the House debates a bill, it utilizes the

   1) Cloture Rule
   2) Five-Minute Rule
   3) Closed Rule
   4) Calendar of General Orders
   5) House Calendar

15. The term of office for the members of the House of Representatives is

   1) 2 years
   2) 3 years
   3) 4 years
   4) 5 years
   5) 6 years.

16. The term of office for the members of the Senate is

   1) 2 years
   2) 3 years
   3) 4 years
   4) 5 years
   5) 6 years.

17.   An immigration bill which allows a specific person to come into this country who would otherwise not be qualified is called a

        1) special resolution
        2) private bill
        3) discharge petition
        4) public bill
        5) private treaty.

18.   If Congress passes a statement urging the Chinese government to become more democratic, such action would be called a

        1) resolution
        2) private bill
        3) congressional order
        4) public bill
        5) treaty.

19.   A bill dealing with increasing income taxes is called a

        1) public bill
        2) private bill
        3) revenue bill
        4) both #1 and #3
        5) both #2 and #3.

20.   In the House, the ___ assigns bills to standing committees.

        1) majority leader
        2) minority leader
        3) majority whip
        4) minority whip
        5) Speaker of the House.

21.   In the Senate, the ___ assigns bills to standing committees

        1) presiding officer
        2) minority leader
        3) majority whip
        4) minority whip
        5) majority leader.

22. In the House of Representatives, the calendar which is used for revenue or appropriations bills is called the

    1) Union Calendar
    2) Consent Calendar
    3) Private Calendar
    4) Discharge Calendar
    5) House Calendar.

23. In the House of Representatives, the calendar which is used for all major, public bills except revenue or appropriations bills is called the

    1) Union Calendar
    2) Consent Calendar
    3) Private Calendar
    4) Discharge Calendar
    5) House Calendar.

24. In the House of Representatives, the calendar which is used for bills arriving on a discharge petition is called the

    1) Union Calendar
    2) Consent Calendar
    3) Calendar of General Orders
    4) Discharge Calendar
    5) House Calendar.

25. In the Senate, the calendar which is used for all public and private bills is called the

    1) Executive Calendar
    2) Consent Calendar
    3) Private Calendar
    4) Discharge Calendar
    5) Calendar of General Orders.

26. The most powerful member of the Senate is usually the

    1) President of the Senate
    2) President Pro Tempore
    3) majority whip
    4) Vice President of the United States
    5) majority leader.

27. Congress uses the _____ Clause of the Constitution in passing legislation that affects most people in the U.S.

    1) Interstate Rendition
    2) Exclusive Powers
    3) Full Faith and Credit
    4) Commerce
    5) Taxation.

28. A bill that has been vetoed can be overridden by a

    1) simple majority of the House and a simple majority of the Senate
    2) two-thirds vote of the Congress as a whole
    3) three-fifths vote of the House and a three-fifths vote of the Senate
    4) two-thirds vote of the House and a simple majority of the Senate.
    5) two-thirds vote of the House and a two-thirds vote of the Senate

29. The President of the Senate

    1) may vote only in case of a tie
    2) is the most powerful member of the Senate
    3) may vote only when a majority of the Senate has voted to have him/her do so
    4) appoints members to the various committees of the Senate
    5) both #1 and #4.

Fill-in-the-Blank Questions

Write the appropriate word or words in the blanks provided.

1. A two-house legislative body is described as _____ .

2. Bills that concern only certain, named individuals are called _____ bills.

3. Bills that concern the internal affairs of either the House or the Senate or that express congressional opinions on something are called _____ .

4. Bills that generally affect everyone in the United States are called _____ bills.

5. _____ rules require that all congressional committee meetings be held in open sessions unless the committee votes to hold closed meetings.

6. The _____ Committee controls the flow of bills to the floor of the House of Representatives.

7. Bills reach the floor of the Senate either by _____ or by _____ .

8. The _____ is a legislative maneuver used in the Senate to delay a vote on a bill for such a long time that the bill will not be voted upon at all.

9. A _____ committee is formed to iron out differences when a bill on some subject has passed the House and the Senate but not in identical form.

10. In the absence of the President of the Senate, the person next in line officially to act as presiding officer of the Senate is the _____ .

11. The President of the Senate also serves as _____ of the United States.

12. Congressional leaders called _____ take unofficial counts of votes before actual voting is done, make sure that party members are present for voting, pressure party members to vote with the party on various issues, etc.

13. When the House Rules Committee sends a bill to the floor of the House as "closed," the bill may not be _____ .

14. When a congressional committee closes its meeting to the public, the committee is said to be in _____ .

15. When the House Rules Committee sends a bill to the floor of the House as "open," the bill may be _____ .

16. A congressional district in which the same representative continues to be re-elected time and again are called _____ districts.

True/False Questions

Write the correct answer in the blanks provided.

1. Senators tend to vote more in line with their parties than do members of the House of Representatives because senators serve longer terms than representatives. _____

2. The number of men and women in Congress is an accurate reflection of the percentage of men and women in American society. _____

3. Because the United States is a pluralist society, very few compromises have to be made in Congress. _____

4. Since discriminatory practices and attitudes have changed, women and minorities now number about half of the members of Congress. _____

5. Because the job is so stressful, members of the House usually do not seek re-election after 2 terms. _____

6. Committees and subcommittees are not really that important since most of the real work is done on the floor of Congress. _____

7. Committee and subcommittee chairpersons are always members of the majority party and usually senior members of the majority party. _____

8. If the House of Representatives wants to consider a bill that a committee has refused to report to the floor, the House members can sign a discharge petition. _____

9. If the Senate wants to consider a bill that a committee has refused to report to the floor, the Senators can pass a special resolution. _____

10. The House and the Senate Rules Committees control the flow of bills to the floor of their respective chambers. _____

11. If the Rules Committee decides not to take action on a bill, then the bill is killed since this committee has complete control over the flow of legislation to the floor of the House. _____

12. Of the two methods by which bills may reach the floor of the Senate, unanimous consent is the preferred method since it avoids lengthy debates. _____

13. Once reported out of committee, a bill may not be amended. _____

14. A member of the House may speak as long as he/she wants to speak unless the cloture rule is invoked. _____

15. The cloture rule is seldom used, even when possible, for fear of angering the legislators who are engaging in a filibuster. _____

16. Presidents, unlike governors in many states, do not possess the authority of the item veto. _____

17. Since Congress overrides most presidential vetoes, the veto is a *not* powerful check on Congress. _____

18. Despite the fact that some of his power has been taken away, the Speaker of the House remains the most powerful figure in the House of Representatives. _____

19. A pocket veto can be overridden just like a regular veto. The only difference is that the override requires a 3/4 majority vote for a pocket veto _____

20. Because the House is more democratic in its procedures it does not utilize the seniority system. _____

21. Members of Congress appointment their staff because of the persons' expertise, *not* because of any political considerations such as campaign contributions. _____

22. Finding information about congressional hearings, votes, and other current congressional activities is relatively easy since the arrival of the Internet. _____

Discussion Questions

Use your own paper to answer the following questions.

1. What is meant by the term *professional politician,* as it relates to members of Congress?

2. Describe the process by which a *revenue* bill would become a law.

3. Explain the options the president has when a bill is sent to him/her after passage by Congress.

4. Explain how the Speaker of the House, the President Pro Tempore of the Senate, the majority and minority floor leaders and whips of the House and the Senate are selected.

5. Discuss the official duties of the committee chairperson in Congress and the chairperson's influence on the outcome of legislation in committee.

6. The record of any conference committee reports only what the committee as a whole decided. What is the significance of this reporting procedure to individual members of the committee?

Using Your Little Gray Cells

1. Find out who represents your state in the United States Senate and who represents your district in the United States House of Representatives. Which congressional district do you live in? (The districts are numbered within each state.) How many terms have your senators and your representative served?

2. Give a summary of demographic data on your state's members of the United States Senate and House of Representatives: previous occupation, previous political experience, religion, ethnic background/nationality, age, sex, race, education.

3. Find out what committees your United States senators and representative serve on. Do they serve as chairperson of any committees or subcommittees?

4. Over a two-week or more period, watch at least two hours of C-SPAN, which covers congressional debates, as well as committee hearings. Be sure that you watch some debates from the House of Representatives and some from the Senate. Compare the two houses regarding the procedures you observed and generally how the sessions appeared to you to be different.

Chapter 11

The American Presidency

In our brief national history, we have shot four of our presidents, worried five of them to death, impeached one and hounded another out of office. And when all else fails, we hold an election and assassinate their character.

P.J. O'Rourke, U.S. journalist

Learning Objectives

After reading and studying the chapter on the executive branch in the text, you should have a better understanding of the following:

1. The formal and informal qualifications of the presidency;
2. How the president and the vice president are elected;
3. What makes a successful president;
4. The transition from one president to the next;
5. What happens when a president becomes disabled;
6. The duties and powers of the president and the vice president and any controversies surrounding their performance;

Chapter Outline

I. Washington
   A. Established many presidential traditions
   B. Co-optation

II. Article II--Qualifications
   A. Age: 35
   B. Native born citizen of United States
   C. Resident of United States for 14 years

III. Informal Qualifications
   A. Male
   B. Caucasian
   C. Fifties
   D. Northern European descent
   E. Christian
   F. Lawyer
   G. Former governor or senator
   H. Married (preferably not divorced)
   I. Ideologically moderate

IV. Election of the President and Length of Term
   A. Electoral college
      a. Intended to make president independent
      b. Exists only one day every four years
      c. Has not produced desired independence
   B. Electoral vote total = 538
   C. Majority required to be elected (270)

V. Term of Office
   A. Four years
   B. Can serve two years of a deceased/resigned president's term
      for a total of 10 years
      1. Tradition of two terms begun by Washington
      2. 22nd Amendment made two terms or ten years mandatory
   C. Recommendations for change
      1. Six years
      2. Ten years

VI. What Makes a "Good" President
   A. Positive attitudes toward the job
   B. Positive attitudes toward people in general
   C. The analysis of James D. Barber
      1. Active/positive
      2. Active/negative
      3. Passive/positive
      4. Passive/negative

VII. Presidential Succession
   A. Vice president becomes president, according to Constitution
      and 25th Amendment
   B. By Law, after vice president come
      1. Speaker of the House
      2. President Pro Tem of the Senate
      3. Secretary of State
      4. Remainder of Cabinet in order in which posts created
   C. Appointment of vice president if vacancy occurs
      1. Provided for in 25th Amendment
      2. Appointed by president with approval of majority of entire Congress

VIII. Presidential Disability
   A. 25th Amendment
   B. President can declare himself disabled
   C. If he can't/doesn't, vice president and majority of Cabinet
      can declare him disabled
   D. If president objects, 2/3 vote of both houses of Congress
      decides

IX. The Vice President
   A. Qualifications and nomination process
      1. Qualifications--same as for president
      2. Usually selected to "balance the ticket"
   B. Duties
      1. Official, i.e., required by Constitution

       a. Preside as President of the Senate

       b. Vote in Senate in case of tie

       c. Wait for president to die, resign, or be removed

    2. Unofficial (with some recent presidents)

       a. Substitute for president on ceremonial occasions

       b. Presidential messenger, fact-finder, goodwill ambassador

       c. Campaigner and spokesperson for administration

       d. Ombudsman

       e. Lobbyist/liaison in Senate

       f. Member of councils, task forces, and forums

       g. Advisor to President

X. Duties of the President

  A. Foreign affairs powers

    1. Commander in chief of armed forces

       a. Use of troops domestically and in foreign countries

       b. War Powers Resolution, 1973

          (1) President can commit troops only after declaration of war by Congress, or by specific authorization by law, or in a national emergency created by attack on United States or its armed forces

          (2) If national emergency, president must report to Congress within 48 hours

          (3) Must remove troops within 60 days unless Congress authorizes them to stay

          (4) Must consult Congress "in every possible instance" before committing troops to battle

          (5) Not particularly effective in curbing president's war-making powers

    2. Treaty-making power

       a. Must have concurrence of 2/3 of Senate

       b. Concurrence of Senate usually granted

       c. Exceptions

          (1) Treaty of Versailles to end World War I

          (2) Strategic Arms Limitation Treaty to limit weapons of United States and former Soviet Union

    3. Executive agreements

       a. Force of treaty

       b. Do not require Senate approval

       c. Not binding on future presidents

       d. Most involve trade matters

       e. Must be reported to Congress within 60 days

       f. About 4 times as many executive agreements as treaties

    4. Extend diplomatic recognition

a. Recognition of another government as legitimate
b. Symbolized by sending and receiving ambassadors
5. Growth of presidential power in foreign affairs
    a. Resulted from nature of office and character of foreign
    b. Grew in proportion to power of U.S.
    c. 9/11 crisis increased power again
B. Legislative Powers
    1. President as chief legislator
        a. State of the Union Address
        b. Budget Message
        c. Economic Message
    2. Prepare national government budget
    3. Regular veto
        a. President lists objections and sends bill back to Congress
        b. Congress can override by 2/3 vote of both houses
    4. Line-item veto
        a. Some governors have it
        b. President does not
        c. Declared unconstitutional for president unless done by amendment
        d. Allows president to veto specific items in bill while signing the remainder into law
    5. Pocket veto
        a. President refuses to sign bill
        b. If Congress not in session within 10 working days, bill dies
    6. Executive orders
        a. Issued by president and have force of law
        b. Many involve filling in details of laws passed by Congress
        c. Examples
            (1) Truman's order to integrate armed forces
            (2) Reagan's order to decontrol price of oil, etc.
    7. Preferment
        a. Granted to president by Congress
        b. Awarding government contracts
        c. Selecting sites of government installations
    8. Party leader
        a. President highly dependent on party in Congress
        b. Must mobilize members of both parties if president's legislative proposals are to succeed

9. President's legislative skills
    a. Legislative log rolling
    b. Pork barrel legislation
    c. Honeymoon period
    d. Priorities
C. The Executive Powers
    1. Appointment and removal power
        a. Many appointments are result of patronage--paying off political debts
        b. Examples
            (1) Diplomats
            (2) Judges
            (3) Cabinet
            (4) Other federal officers
        c. Most require consent of 2/3 of Senate
            (1) Senate usually concurs with no problems
            (2) Sometimes Senate rejects nominee
            (3) Senatorial courtesy
        d. Removal of officials fundamental to presidential success
    2. Financial power
        a. Delegated by Congress
        b. Create budget
        c. Discretionary spending
    3. Law enforcement power
        a. Enforces congressional acts
        b. Enforces court orders
D. Enforce laws of United States
E. Judicial functions
    1. Examples
        a. Executive clemency (pardons)
        b. Amnesties
        c. Reprieves
        d. Commutations
    2. Apply only to federal crimes
    3. May not pardon persons impeached

XII. Conclusion

Important Terms

Presidential succession
Balance the ticket
Pork barrel legislation
Amnesty
Patronage
Executive agreement
Economic Message
Regular veto
Executive orders
State of the Union
  Message
Salt II

Article II
Presidential disability
War Powers Resolution
Legislative log rolling
Diplomatic recognition
Senatorial courtesy
Budget Message
Pocket veto
Preferment
Budget and Accounting
  Act of 1921
Geraldine Ferarro

Co-optation
"Honeymoon" period
Commander in Chief
Reprieve
The Cabinet
Electoral College
Line-item veto
Executive clemency
Commutation
Twenty-fifth
  Amendment

Multiple Choice Questions

Circle the number of the correct answer.

1. The term of office of the president and the vice president is

    (1) two years
    (2) eight years
    (3) four years
    (4) five years
    (5) ten years.

2. The maximum number of <u>terms</u> a president may serve is
    (1) one term
    (2) two terms
    (3) three terms
    (4) four terms
    (5) an unlimited number of terms.

3. The maximum number of <u>years</u> a president may serve is

    (1) two years
    (2) four years
    (3) five years
    (4) ten years
    (5) an unlimited number of years.

14th edition

4. The issue of the vice president's "becoming" president in the event that the presidency is vacant was clarified in

    (1) Amendment 19
    (2) Amendment 23
    (3) Amendment 24
    (4) Amendment 25
    (5) Amendment 26.

5. The first vice president of the United States forced to resign his office was

    (1) Aaron Burr
    (2) Thomas Jefferson
    (3) Spiro Agnew
    (4) Richard Nixon
    (5) Walter Mondale.

6. The first president of the United States to resign his office was

    (1) Richard Nixon
    (2) Gerald Ford
    (3) Thomas Jefferson
    (4) Jimmy Carter
    (5) Dwight Eisenhower.

7. The 25th Amendment of the Constitution deals with

    (1) Presidential disability
    (2) Presidential succession
    (3) Appointment of a vice president
    (4) both 1 and 2
    (5) all--1, 2, and 3.

8. The Supreme Court ordered the desegregation of public schools in

    (1) *Marbury v. Madison*
    (2) *Gibbons v. Ogden*
    (3) *Brown v. Board of Education*
    (4) *Murray v. Baltimore*
    (5) *Plessy v. Ferguson.*

9. The Executive Branch of the United States government is discussed in the Constitution in

    (1) Article 1
    (2) Article 2
    (3) Article 3
    (4) Article 4
    (5) Article 5.

10. The group of people who actually elect the president and the vice president is the

    (1) state legislatures
    (2) electoral college
    (3) Congress
    (4) Supreme Court
    (5) Senate.

11. The number of votes from this group currently required to be elected to the offices of president and vice president is

    (1) 275
    (2) 371
    (3) 535
    (4) 538
    (5) 270.

12. The amendment to the Constitution that prohibits the president from serving an unlimited number of terms is

    (1) Amendment 21
    (2) Amendment 22
    (3) Amendment 23
    (4) Amendment 24
    (5) Amendment 25.

13. The first appointed vice president was

    (1) Thomas Jefferson
    (2) Aaron Burr
    (3) Richard Nixon
    (4) Nelson Rockefeller
    (5) Gerald Ford.

14. When a vice president is appointed by the president to fill a vacancy in the office, he/she must be approved by a majority of

    (1) the state legislatures
    (2) the Cabinet
    (3) the Senate
    (4) the House of Representatives
    (5) both the House and the Senate.

15. The first woman nominated for vice president by a major party in the United States was

    (1) Pat Schroeder
    (2) Geraldine Ferarro
    (3) Shirley Chisolm
    (4) Gloria Steinem
    (5) Phyllis Schlafly.

16. According to the Constitution, the authority to declare war belongs to the

    (1) President
    (2) House of Representatives
    (3) Senate
    (4) House and the Senate combined
    (5) President and a majority of his/her Cabinet.

17. The President shares his/her authority to "make" treaties with the

    (1) the Cabinet
    (2) the House of Representatives
    (3) the Senate
    (4) both the House and the Senate
    (5) the Supreme Court.

18. Most of the appointments that a president makes must be approved by

    (1) the Cabinet
    (2) the House of Representatives
    (3) the Senate
    (4) both the House and the Senate
    (5) the Supreme Court.

19. The presidential address in which the president discusses the problems of the country and makes some general legislative suggestions for solving these problems is called the

    (1) Budget Message
    (2) State of the Union Address
    (3) Economic Message
    (4) Annual Report of the President of the United States
    (5) none of the above.

20. The <u>specific</u> term used to denote a group pardon is

    (1) commutation
    (2) amnesty
    (3) a stay of execution
    (4) executive clemency
    (5) reprieve.

21. A delay in the execution of a sentence is called

    (1) commutation
    (2) amnesty
    (3) a stay of execution
    (4) executive clemency
    (5) reprieve.

22. The reduction of a sentence is called

    (1) commutation
    (2) amnesty
    (3) a stay of execution
    (4) executive clemency
    (5) reprieve.

23. The president's authority in the area of executive clemency extends <u>only</u> to people who are involved in

    (1) serious crimes like murder
    (2) state crimes
    (3) federal crimes
    (4) crimes against property
    (5) treason.

14th edition

24. When a president makes an appointment to pay off a political debt, the appointment is said to be one based on

   (1) merit
   (2) preferment
   (3) patronage
   (4) executive privilege
   (5) amnesty.

25. The period of time right after a president is first elected in which Congress is more cooperative than they might be later on is called the _____ period.

   (1) preferment
   (2) doldrum
   (3) paradise
   (4) honeymoon
   (5) innocent.

26. When a president persuades political enemies to join his/her Cabinet, for example, so their criticisms will be silenced, such an action is referred to as

   (1) preferment
   (2) a political payoff
   (3) executive privilege
   (4) co-optation
   (5) patronage.

Fill-in-the-Blank Questions

Write the appropriate word or words in the blanks provided.

1. What are the formal qualifications for the offices of President and Vice President of the United States?

   (1) _____
   (2) _____
   (3) _____

2. By the use of _____ the president can "get around" the constitutional requirement that the Senate approve agreements made by the president with foreign countries. 3.   What have been some of the "unofficial" duties of the vice president in recent years under some presidents?

(1) _____

(2) _____

(3) _____

(4) _____

3.   The major advisory role of the vice president occurs as a member of what two groups in the executive branch?

(1) _____

(2) _____

4.   What is the order of presidential succession after the vice president?

(1) _____

(2) _____

(3) _____

(4) _____

5.   What two notable treaties did the Senate refuse to ratify and what did they deal with?

(1) _____

(2) _____

7.   Name two countries listed in your text to which the United States does _not_ extend diplomatic recognition?

(1) _____   (2) _____

8.   What are the 4 major provisions of the War Powers Resolution, 1973?

(1) _____
_____

(2) _____
_____

(3) _____
_____

(4) _____
_____

14th edition

9. The term _____ means that the selection of vice-presidential nominees is based more on their demographic characteristics than on their ability to perform the duties of president, if they were to become president.

10. The _____ requires the president to present to Congress a budget for the national government every year.

11. According to the Constitution, what are the official duties of the vice president besides taking over for the president if necessary?

    (1) _____
    (2) _____

12. The president addresses Congress annually concerning some specific national problems related to the economy and to specific budget proposals. These addresses are called the _____ and the _____, respectively.

13. Issued by the president, _____ have the same effect as if they were laws passed by the legislative branch.

14. The president's authority to decide which companies will build the space shuttle and to select the sites of air bases, for example, is called _____.

15. A legislative maneuver characterized as "You scratch my back and I'll scratch yours" is called _____.

16. _____ is legislation designed to bring construction dollars to a particular district for such things as river and harbor projects, highway construction, new post offices, etc.

True/False Questions

Write *true* if the statement is completely true; write *false* if the statement is in any way false.

1. The Constitution makes it clear that the president has the sole authority to make foreign policy. _____

2. The president's authority as commander in chief of the armed forces is unlimited. _____

3. The Framers of the Constitution conceived of the president's role as commander in chief as one of independent political authority. _____

4. In recent times United States presidents have been much less inclined to send American troops to fight on foreign soil than presidents were in earlier times. _____

5. Since the 1970s, American presidents have argued that they had implied, but concurrent, powers in the area of foreign affairs. _____

6. Presidents have been very willing to use troops domestically to curb riots, for example, since the state and city government officials have always been enthusiastic supporters of the president's authority in this area. _____

7. The U.S. government is this country's largest single buyer of goods and services. _____

8. Most executive agreements cover major issues with foreign governments because the president does not want to have to argue with the Senate over a treaty. _____

9. The Case Act requires that the president notify Congress within 60 days if the president plans to leave troops in a foreign country without a declaration of war. _____

10. The United States usually acquires embassies by treaty arrangement so that the embassy grounds can become American soil. _____

11. The president cannot extend diplomatic recognition without the consent of the Senate. _____

12. In reporting his use of an executive agreement, the president can report to the Senate Foreign Relations Committee and the House International Relations Committee instead of the full Congress. _____

Discussion Questions

Use your own paper to answer the following questions.

1. Construct an argument in favor of changing the president's term of office to a term longer than what is served now. (To answer this question, state what length of term a president serves now and why that term is too short. How long should the term be? What problems would that longer term solve? Under your proposal, should the President's terms of office be limited? If so, how and why?)

2. Discuss the characteristics and behavior styles you think a president should have to be a "good" president. Give reasons to back up your answer. (You should consider his/her personal qualities, how he/she should deal with Congress and with the bureaucracy, how much control he/she should utilize in getting things done, etc.)

3. Based on your knowledge of the American political-party system and the way presidents and vice presidents are elected, why are vice presidents often selected merely to "balance the ticket.? (To answer this question well, you must define the term "balance the ticket" and explain how it relates to getting a president elected. You must show how "balancing the ticket" relates to the types of major parties the United States has and to the method of electing the chief executive.)

4. What are the provisions of the War Powers Resolution? Using a part or parts of the Constitution, construct an argument that one of these provisions is unconstitutional. (Be sure you identify which provision you are claiming is unconstitutional and the part or parts of the Constitution you are using.)

5. List and explain the constitutional duties of the vice president. Name and explain at least three "unofficial" duties of the vice president. Why do you suppose the writers of the Constitution did not give the vice president a larger "official" role in the government?

Using Your Little Gray Cells

1. Find out what caused the United States to break diplomatic relations with one or more of the following countries: Albania, Angola, Cambodia, or Cuba.

2. Presidents have granted amnesty to draft evaders and deserters after other wars besides the Vietnam War. Find out which ones, when the war ended, when the president granted the amnesty, and if there was any serious disagreement over his granting of the amnesty.

3. The president has the power to extend diplomatic recognition or to withhold it from any country he/she desires. Most presidents have been very "flexible" about who gets recognized and who doesn't. Assume that the president is thinking about whether or not to continue diplomatic relations with the People's Republic of China (Communist China). You are the president's foreign policy advisor, and the president has asked you to express your opinion in writing about continuing or discontinuing diplomatic relations with China, giving your reasons. (Your job rides on how good your advice is!)

4. Compare and contrast the role of the President of the United States as head of the government to the role of the president of a large, multi-national corporation such as IBM. Should presidents be more like their corporate counterparts or not? Explain.

157
Chapter 11

Chapter 12

The Executive Bureaucracy

Learning Objectives

After reading and studying the chapter on the challenges to American democracy, you should have a better understanding of the following:

1. The meaning, functions, and organization of the bureaucracy;
2. The functions of the civil service merit system;
3. How one obtains employment with the federal government;
4. How federal employees are classified and compensated;
5. Positive and negative aspects of the bureaucracy.
6. The importance of the bureaucracy.

Outline

I. Introduction
    A. Executive bureaucracy: administrative units that carry out the day-to-day activities of executive branch
    B. Four large groupings
       1. The Executive Office of the President
       2. The Cabinet
       3. Independent agencies and regulatory commissions
       4. Government corporations
    C. Size
       1. About 3 million civilian employees
       2. Over a million military employees
    D. Distribution
       1. Nearly 83% work outside D.C.
       2. 4% work abroad
    E. Reasons for Bureaucratic Expansion
       1. Increased population; complex society
       2. Public acceptance of government regulations in private sector
       3. Public acceptance of welfare programs
       4. Bureaucracy's tendency to expand indefinitely

II. How the Federal Executive Bureaucracy is Organized
    A. The Executive Office of the President
       1. Major officers appointed by president with consent of Senate
       2. Serve at his pleasure
       3. Collection of agencies that provide president with advice, assistance, and coordinated effort in various fields
       4. Major agencies
          a. White House Office
             (1) Speech writers
             (2) Press Secretary
             (3) National Security Advisor

159

Chapter 12

14th Edition

        (4) Congressional Liaison
        (5) Appointment Secretary
        (6) Chief Economic Advisor
        (7) White House Chief of Staff
    b. Office of Management and the Budget (OMB)
        (1) Assists President in preparing budget
        (2) Helps get budget enacted into law
    c. Council of Economic Advisors
        (1) Advises President on economic matters
        (2) Prepares reports forecasting economy
    d. National Security Council
        (1) Advises president on matters of national security
        (2) Consists of the following
           (a) President
           (b) Vice president
           (c) Secretary of State
           (d) Secretary of Defense
           (e) CIA Director
           (f) Chairman of Joint Chiefs of Staff
           (g) Anyone else the president wants
    e. Office of United States Trade Representative
        (1) Develops and carries out foreign trade polices of United States
        (2) Headed by United States Trade Representative
    f. Office of National Drug Control Policy
        (1) Created in 1988
        (2) Prepares a national drug control strategy and makes recommendations to the president on organization, management and the budgets of federal departments and agencies dealing with drug enforcement
    g. Office of National AIDS Policy
        (1) Coordinating domestic efforts to reduce the number of new cases
        (2) Created during Clinton Administration
B. The Cabinet
  1. Appointed by president with approval of 2/3 of Senate
  2. Serve as long as president wants them
  3. Typical Cabinet members
    a. Secretary of State
    b. Secretary of Defense
    c. Secretary of the Treasury
    d. Secretary of the Interior
    e. Secretary of Agriculture
    f. Secretary of Commerce
    g. Secretary of Labor
    h. Secretary of Health and Human Services
    i. Secretary of Housing and Urban Development

          j.   Secretary of Transportation
          k. Secretary of Energy
          l.   Secretary of Education
         m. Secretary of Veterans Affairs
          n. Secretary of Homeland Security
          o. Attorney General (Department of Justice)
          p. Vice president

4. Obama includes the Budget Director, the United Nations Ambassador, White House Chief of Staff, head of Environmental Protection Agency, and U.S. Trade Representative

C. Independent agencies
1. Most do not belong to any Cabinet department
2. Agency members appointed by president with consent 2/3 of Senate
3. Agency members usually serve fixed terms of office
4. Cannot be fired except for demonstrated cause
5. Examples
   a. General Accounting Office
   b. Office of Personnel Management
   c. Environmental Protection Agency

D. "Independent" Regulatory Commissions
1. Regulate various phases of private business activities
2. Quasi-legislative and quasi-judicial authority
3. Commission members appointed by president with consent of 2/3 of Senate
4 Members usually serve fixed terms of office
5. Cannot be fired except for demonstrated cause
6. Examples
   a. Federal Reserve Board
   b. Federal Trade Commission
   c. Food and Drug Administration
   d. Federal Communications Commission
   e. Securities and Exchange Commission
   f. National Labor Relations Board
   g. Occupational Health and Safety Administration (OSHA)
   h. Consumer Product Safety Commission
   i. Nuclear Regulatory Commission
   j. United States International Trade Commission
   k. Federal Energy Regulatory Commission

E. Government Corporations
1. Government-owned businesses created to provide some service at reduced cost or free to consumer
2. Examples
   a. Tennessee Valley Authority (TVA)
   b. United States Postal Service
   c. Federal Deposit Insurance Corporation (FDIC)
   d. Amtrak

F. Civil Service

1. "Spoils" System (Patronage)
    a. Associated with President Andrew Jackson
    b. Appointing friends and supporters instead of most qualified persons
2. Merit System
    a. Pendleton Act, 1883
        (1) Created the Civil Service Commission
        (2) Now called Office of Personnel Management (OPM)
    b. Hiring based on "merit"
        (1) competitive exams
        (2) education
        (3) work experience
    c. Covers over 90% of all national-government jobs
    d. President still has many patronage jobs to hand out
    e. Terminating employment of merit-system civil servants difficult
3. Reforms
    a. Merit pay
    b. Government in the Sunshine Act
    c. Sunset laws
    d. Civil Service Reform Act, 1978
4. Bureaucracy unlikely to shrink in light of huge government programs under Obama administration.

III. Employment with the Federal Government
    A. Critics urge drastic change
    B. Individual agencies usually do the hiring
    C. OPM does the following assists in some ways
    D. Most jobs are merit-system positions
    E. Examples of exempted services--non-competitive
        1. CIA
        2. Defense Intelligence Agency
        3. Secret Service--Uniformed Branch
        4. FBI
        5. Federal Reserve System--Board of Governors
        6. Library of Congress
        7. U.S. Nuclear Regulatory Commission
        8. General Accounting Office
        9. National Security Agency
    F. Exempted positions
        1. Teachers in overseas schools for military dependents
        2. Medical personnel in Dept. of Veterans Affairs
        3. National Science Foundation scientists and engineers
        4. Drug enforcement agents
    G. Classification and Compensation
        1. General Schedule (GS)

Chapter 12

                    a. Salary schedule and job classification for most
                        "white-collar" federal jobs
                    b. Ranges from GS-1 to GS-15
                2. Federal Wage System (WG)
                    a. Salary schedule and job classification for some
                        "blue-collar" workers
                    b. Salary varies according to geographic area
                3. Senior management positions paid on different schedule
                    ranging from EX-1 to EX-5
        H. Examinations
                1. Some positions require a test
                    a. Typist
                    b. Many post office jobs
                    c. Foreign Service Officers
                2. Some merely require a resume

IV.   The Role of the Bureaucracy
        A. Implementation function
                1. Carries out programs of government
                2. Problems
                    a. Faulty program design
                    b. Lack of clear directions
                    c. Inadequate resources
                    d. Bureaucratic red tape
                    e. Bureaucrats who have minds of their own
                    f. Decentralization
                    g. Capture
        B. The Regulatory Function
                1. Cost benefit ratio questioned
                2. American lives regulated much more than people think

V.   Conclusions
        A. Some regulation necessary
        B. Bureaucracy will expand
        C. Danger: who controls the regulators?

Important Terms

Executive Office of the President
Office of Management and the Budget
Quaisi-legislative authority
National Security Council
Office of the Vice President
General Accounting Office
Government corporation
Office of Personnel Management
Independent regulatory commission
Merit Systems Protection Board
Quasi-judicial authority
Civil Service Reform Act
Government in the Sunshine Act

Patronage
Independent agency
Federal Wage System
Bureaucracy
Merit system
Exempted positions
The White House Office
Exempted services
FDIC
Sunset laws
Whistleblower
Capture

Multiple Choice Questions

Circle the number of the correct choice.

1. The executive agency within the Executive Office of the President, which consists of about 500 people who are the president's closest advisors, is the

    (1) The Office of Policy Development
    (2) Office of Management and the Budget
    (3) Council of Economic Advisors
    (4) White House Office
    (5) National Security Council.

2. The executive agency within the Executive Office of the President which is responsible for advising the president about economic matters and for preparing reports forecasting the long- and short-term behavior of the economy is the

    (1) Office of Policy Development
    (2) Office of Management and the Budget
    (3) Council of Economic Advisors
    (4) White House Office
    (5) Office of Policy Development.

14th Edition

3. The executive agency within the Executive Office of the President that was heavily involved in the Iran-Contra scandal of the 1980s was the

    (1) Office of Policy Development
    (2) National Security Council
    (3) Council of Economic Advisors
    (4) White House Office
    (5) Office of Policy Development.

4. One of the major criticisms of the Office of National Drug Control Policy is that

    (1) drug enforcement is too costly
    (2) the agency is corrupt
    (3) the agency does not have enough control over drug enforcement/policy
    (4) "street" drugs should be made legal so there would be no need for such an agency
    (5) the president appoints the "drug czar" as a patronage appointment and not under the merit system.

5. The president's Cabinet began under the presidency of

    (1) George Washington
    (2) Abraham Lincoln
    (3) Harry Truman
    (4) Franklin Roosevelt
    (5) Thomas Jefferson.

6. Members of the president's Cabinet serve

    (1) unlimited terms of office
    (2) at the pleasure of the president
    (3) fixed terms of office which coincide with the president's
    (4) two-year terms of office
    (5) at the pleasure of the Congress.

7. Which one of the following is an independent agency?

    (1) the GAO
    (2) the Postal Service
    (3) the Federal Reserve Board
    (4) the National Labor Relations Board
    (5) the TVA.

8. Which one of the following is an independent regulatory commission?

   (1) The General Accounting Office
   (2) The Postal Service
   (3) The Office of Personnel Management
   (4) The National Labor Relations Board
   (5) The Tennessee Valley Authority.

9. Which one of the following is a government corporation?

   (1) the GAO
   (2) the Securities and Exchange Commission
   (3) the OPM
   (4) the National Labor Relations Board
   (5) the TVA.

10. Which one of the following was created to provide inexpensive hydroelectric power for parts of the United States

   (1) the GAO
   (2) the FDIC
   (3) the OPM
   (4) the SEC
   (5) the TVA.

11. Since the 1980s much of the hiring authority of the executive bureaucracy has been delegated to

   (1) private employment agencies
   (2) state-run employment agencies
   (3) individual agencies in the federal government
   (4) the Office of Personnel Management
   (5) the White House Office.

12. All but one of the following are considered "exempted positions" in the national bureaucracy. Which one is not?

   (1) teachers in overseas schools for dependents of the Department of Defense
   (2) positions in the Office of Personnel Management
   (3) medical personnel in the Department of Veterans Affairs
   (4) drug enforcement agents
   (5) engineers with the National Science Foundation.

14th Edition

13. In the context of the bureaucracy, a (an) _____ is a government worker who reports egregious governmental inefficiency or illegal activity.

    (1) punker
    (2) squealer
    (3) bureaucrat
    (4) whistleblower
    (5) invisible man.

Fill-in-the-Blank Questions

Write the appropriate word or words in the blanks provided.

1. Those agencies and commissions and other personnel who assist the president in the day-to-day operations of the government are referred to as the_____.

2. What are the two primary tasks of the OMB?

    (1) _____
    (2) _____

3. The tendency of an agency to develop a very close relationship with the special interests it oversees is referred to as _____.

4. Agencies in the executive branch which are usually not part of the Cabinet because they don't really fit in any department, or because Congress wanted them to be separated, or because they perform a service for many or all departments are called _____.

5. Those federal government agencies that fall outside the jurisdiction of the OPM are called _____ services.

6. Most "white-collar" positions with the national government are classified and paid according something called the _____ _____.

7. Some "blue-collar" workers are classified and paid according to something called the _____.

8. Many positions with the federal government bureaucracy require that the prospective employee merely submit a _____.

9. The two functions of the executive bureaucracy are the _____ function and the _____ function.

10. Many Independent Agencies and Independent Regulatory Commissions make rules and adjudicate their rules; therefore, they are said to possess _____-legislative authority and _____ - _____ authority.

11. _____ laws allow federal government programs to end at a specific time unless Congress reauthorizes them.

12. The _____ requires that about fifty government agencies hold most of their meetings in public

True/False Questions

Write the correct response in the blank provided.

1. No matter who is president, there are always just 14 Cabinet positions. _____

2. During any president's term of office, the members of the Cabinet change frequently. _____

3. The president's Cabinet has always been the major advisory body of the president. _____

4. The majority of positions with the national government are considered competitive positions. _____

5. The national government has a single employment agency--the Office of Personnel Management. _____

6. Pollution problems in the United States are strictly of our own making. _____

7. All federal government positions require that prospective employees take an examination to prove that they can perform the job. _____

8. Recruiting highly qualified people for the federal bureaucracy is a relatively easy task since so many people are unemployed. ___

9. Salaries in the executive bureaucracy are always equal to or better than in the private sector. _____

10. Because they know they are doing an important job, morale in the bureaucracy is high. _____

11. The federal executive bureaucracy is characterized by decentralization. _____

168
Chapter 12

12. One of the problems of implementing government policy results from laws that are not clear. _____

Discussion Questions

Use your own paper to answer the following questions.

1. Read at least three different sources on the subject of the failure of the bureaucracy at all levels during and after Hurricane Katrina. Pick any problem you discovered with how the bureaucracy failed to perform and write a 500-word essay about how you would solve this particular problem. Be sure to run a spell checker before you submit your essay.

2. Discuss the role of the General Accounting Office. What do you think could be done to eliminate more government waste?

3. What is the civil service merit system designed to do and why?

4. What does the term *patronage* mean? Should it be eliminated? Explain your reasoning.

5. One of the criticisms raised about government bureaucrats is that they are too difficult to fire. What do you think based on the rules in Table 12.4 in your text?

The Federal Government in Cyberspace

Office of Personnel Management

http://www.opm.gov/

Lists employment opportunities with the national government.

FedWorld

http://www.fedworld.gov

A doorway to most federal agencies and sources of information about the national government. FedWorld is a good beginning for any inquiry about the federal government.

Federal Register

http://www.gpoaccess.gov/fr/

Official publication for presidential documents and executive orders. Also includes notices, rules and proposed rules from federal agencies.

Government Manual

http://www.gpoaccess.gov/gmanual/

Descriptions of the functions, organization, and important officials of every federal department and agency. Also includes organizational charts for most.

Using Your Little Gray Cells

1. Think about your daily life. First, create your own scenario--similar to the one presented in the text--which illustrates how government regulates your life. Second, do you think there is too much or too little regulation today? Why?

2. Should the private sector be held to the same dismissal procedures as those of the civil service Merit System? Explain your reasoning. If we were to pass laws requiring these same procedures for the private sector, what impact would this change have on private sector morale? Productivity? Its ability to attract new investment capital?

3. The United States government owns about one-third of all the land in the country. For what reason? Is the reason valid? Explain.

4. The Office of Management and the Budget was created in 1970 to replace the old Bureau of the Budget. One of its primary jobs is to assist the President in preparing the national budget. To do so requires that the group estimate the amount of revenue (mainly from taxes) the national government will have in the budget year and then to allocate that money among various programs such as defense, research on disease prevention, education, etc.

5. One of the major problems facing the United States today, according to some critics, is reducing the national debt, which is the amount of money the United States government owes various countries, financial institutions, and the American public who buy government securities.

   It seems easy to "fix" this problem merely by spending only the amount of money that the government will receive in revenue. However, what will be cut?

What will be eliminated altogether? What interest groups might be involved, i.e., who will be "mad" and who will be glad? Should the budget be developed strictly on the basis of "greatest good for the greatest number," balancing the budget, or should there be other considerations?

Assume you are in the OMB. Decide how the government's revenue should be distributed for the coming fiscal year. For purposes of this exercise, you will assume that the total government revenue will be $100 and that the current national debt to be $400. Interest on the national debt must be paid, and $14.00 has already been set aside for that purpose as you can see on the chart. You are to submit a budget to the president by (1) ranking your budget priorities and (2) designating dollar amounts for each of the categories. However, you may decide to eliminate some of the categories or add others. (The total should be $100, including the $30.00 for interest on the national debt. Be sure that your #1 choice also has the largest amount of money spent on it.)

Budget Item	Rank	Dollar Amount
Health care	____	_____
Environment	____	_____
Defense	____	_____
Crime Prevention	____	_____
Crime Detection	____	_____
Social Security	____	_____
National Debt Principal	____	_____
National Debt Interest	____	$30.00
Foreign Economic Aid	____	_____
Public Housing	____	_____
Job Retraining/Education	____	_____
Roads/Bridges	____	_____
Student Loans	____	_____
Mass Transit (Buses, trains, etc.)	____	_____
AIDS Research	____	_____
Child Care	____	_____
Food Stamps	____	_____
Space Exploration	____	_____

Place a check mark by any taxes you might raise (if any).

Add national sales tax ____   Income tax ____   Alcohol taxes ____
Gasoline tax ____   Cigarette taxes ____

Next Page

What interest groups might oppose your taxes increases (if any)? (Give specific names.)

_____

_____

Why did you choose your first two priorities?

_____

_____

_____

_____

_____

_____

_____

What interest groups might support your first two priorities? (Give specific names.)

_____

_____

What interest groups might oppose your first two priorities? (Give specific names.)

_____

_____

What interest groups might support your taxes increases (if any)? (Give specific names.)

_____

_____

It is our true policy to steer clear of permanent alliances
with any portion of the foreign world.
George Washington, 1796

Speak softly and carry a big stick.
Theodore Roosevelt, 1901

Let us never negotiate out of fear.
But let us never fear to negotiate.
John F. Kennedy, 1961

My attitude is you take preemptive action in order to
protect the American people, that you act in
order to make this country secure.
George W. Bush, 2004

CHAPTER 13

THE RELATIONS OF NATIONS:
THE SHRINKING GLOBE

After reading and studying the chapter on foreign policy, you should have a better understanding of the following:

1. The meaning and objective of foreign policy
2. The tools of foreign policy
3. The patterns of foreign policy
4. The reasons countries go to war
5. The future outlook

Chapter Outline

I. Types of Government Policy
   A. Domestic
   B. Foreign

II. Foreign policy
   A. Country's national interest pursued abroad
   B. Distinction between domestic and foreign policy often blurred
      1. Farm subsidies
      2. Protectionism
      3. Global competition
      4. Interdependency

III. Objective of Foreign Policy: National Self-Preservation
   A. Preserving sovereignty
      1. International law
         a. Treaties agreed to over many centuries
         b. Hugo Grotius
      2. Often violated
   B. Preserving system of government
   C. Preserving ideology
   D. Maintaining physical security
      1. Bilateral treaties
      2. Multilateral treaties
   E. Maintaining economic security
      1. Embargoes
      2. Tariffs
      3. Quotas
      4. Free trade
      5. Most favored nation
      6. NAFTA
      7. Zero-sum game
IV. "Tools" of Foreign Policy
   A. Diplomacy
      1. Communication between governments to convince, confuse,

propagandize, or embarrass
    2. Purposes
        a. Gain something without war
        b. Gain something prior to war
        c. Gain time to prepare for war
        d. Save as much as possible for country if war
           impossible, too risky, or already lost
        e. Divide "spoils" if victorious in war
        f. Make truces during war
        g. Gain other side's point of view
  B. Economics
    1. Protecting domestic industries with tariffs
    2. Developing new industries, products, and technologies
    3. Securing raw materials
    4. Reducing imports
    5. Expanding export markets
    6. Damaging or destroying other countries economically
    7. Establishing economic alliances or empires
    8. Providing foreign aid
  C. Propaganda
    1. Use of words, pictures, and/or actions to promote an
       ideology or policy
    2. Subversion: propaganda designed to weaken or destroy
       "enemy"
  D. Military
    1. Purposes of war
        a. Designed to eliminate real or potential danger
        b. World War II
    2. Targeted warfare
        a. Confined to specific geographic area
        b. Middle East, Kosovo
    3. Surrogate warfare
        a. Using another country's military or rebels rather than your
           own military
        b. Cuba used by Soviets in Angola
        c. Contras used by United States in Nicaragua
    4. Balance of Power
        a. Each side armed equally with deadly weapons
        b. Each side afraid to attack the other
        c. Military budget decreasing in developed countries, but not in
           less developed
    5. Peace Dividend
    6. International terrorism
        a. Definitions vary
        b. Premeditated, politically motivated violence against
           "civilians" involving the citizens or territory of more than one
           country

   c. Not currently threat to existing governments

   d. Types of terrorists

    • Criminals

    • Crazies

    • Crusaders

V. Patterns of Foreign Policy

 A. Isolationism

  1. Country's refusal to become involved externally

  2. United States 1919-1939

  3. Difficult, if not impossible, to achieve today

 B. Neutrality

  1. Non-belligerency, non-active involvement, taking no sides

  2. Argentina during World War II

  3. Specific to a particular conflict

  4. Can be imposed by other country or countries

 E. Diplomatic and judicial accommodation

  1. Foreign policy aimed at solving problems by direct talks or by mediation from another group or country

  2. Both sides must agree to mediation for this pattern to work

  3. World Court

 F. Social, economic, and cultural cooperation

  1. Involves two or more countries recognizing and pursuing common goals

  2. Can be accomplished through

   a. International organizations such as United Nations, International Postal Union, or World Health Organization

   b. Bilateral agreements--between two countries

   c. Multilateral agreements--among three or more countries

   d. Non-governmental organizations (NGOs)

    (1) International Red Cross

    (2) International Chamber of Commerce

 G. Balance of Power

  1. Produced by fear of war

  2. Country shifts allegiance from side to side hoping to create a balance of power between two belligerent countries or groups of countries

  3. Variation: appeasement

  4. Practiced by British until 1939

 H. Collective security

  • Countries join together and pool their resources to increase their individual strengths

 I. Balance of Power: each side armed heavily so neither side wants to attack the other

  • Practiced by former Soviet Union and United States since WW II

 J. Conflict

  1. Does not mean failure of foreign policy; it is a policy itself

2. Can take several forms
   a. Mob violence
   b. Guerrilla warfare
   c. Targeted warfare
   d. Conventional war
   e. Nuclear war
3. Reasons for war
   a. Usually produces fast results
   b. Results usually permanent
   c. Enhances prestige of winner
   d. Ends "cold wars"
   e. Strengthens social "glue" that holds country together
   f. Strengthens the position of the rulers
   g. Provides an excuse for eliminating anyone in country who wishes to overthrow government

VI. A Future
   A. "New world order"
   B. Continuing problems
      1. Destructive nationalism
      2. Uneven distribution of resources
      3. Environmental concerns

Important Terms

Appeasement

Most favored nation trade status

Diplomatic & judicial accommodation

Social, economic, & cultural cooperation

World Trade Organization

Multinational corporations

Zero-sum game

European Union

"New world order"

Hugo Grotius

Multilateral treaties

Surrogate warfare

Balance of power

Neutrality

Terrorism

Collective security

Warsaw Pact

United Nations

International law

Foreign policy

Protectionism

Sovereignty

Bilateral treaties

Targeted warfare

Subversion

Peace dividend

Propaganda

Quotas

Tariff

NATO

NAFTA

Free trade

Ideology

Foreign aid

Embargoes

Diplomacy

Isolationism

World Court

Multiple Choice Questions
Circle the number of the correct answer.

1. _____ is a variation on the pattern of foreign policy, *balance of power.* It involves meeting some of the "enemy's" demands in hopes of avoiding war.

    (1) appellation
    (2) atonement
    (3) appeasement
    (4) rapprochement
    (5) referencing

2. Communism, capitalism, and nationalism are all examples of

    (1) systems of government
    (2) economic systems
    (3) ideologies
    (4) foreign policies
    (5) interventionism.

3. An embargo is one country's

    (1) refusal to buy or sell to another country
    (2) tax on imported goods
    (3) tax on exported goods
    (4) restriction on the quantity of an imported product
    (5) arrangement whereby it agrees to sell products to another country at a cheaper price than it will sell the same product to other countries.

4. In international relations a quota refers to one country's

    (1) refusal to buy or sell to another country
    (2) tax on imported goods
    (3) tax on exported goods
    (4) restriction on the quantity of an imported product
    (5) arrangement whereby it agrees to sell products to another country at a cheaper price than it will sell the same product to other countries.

5. A tariff is one country's

    (1) refusal to buy or sell to another country
    (2) tax on imported goods
    (3) tax on exported goods
    (4) restriction on the quantity of an imported product
    (5) arrangement whereby it agrees to sell products to another country at a cheaper price than it will sell the same product to other countries.

14th Edition

6. The 1973-74 Arab oil embargo is an example of

    (1) diplomacy as a tool of foreign policy
    (2) propaganda as a tool of foreign policy
    (3) the military as a tool of foreign policy
    (4) economics as a tool of foreign policy
    (5) international terrorism as a tool of foreign policy.

7. A prominent economic alliance that has become a real force in the world economy is

    (1) NATO
    (2) the Warsaw Pact
    (3) European Union
    (4) the Alliance for Progress
    (5) the United Nations.

8. Probably the most widely recognized tool of foreign policy is

    (1) economics
    (2) the military
    (3) propaganda
    (4) diplomacy
    (5) international terrorism.

9. The foreign policy pattern that refers to a refusal to become involved with the rest of world or with the region in which the country is located is called

    (1) isolationism
    (2) neutrality
    (3) neutralism
    (4) neutralization
    (5) collective security.

10. The foreign policy pattern which results from a feeling of physical danger from another country or group or a feeling that it can defeat its enemy and still survive is generally referred to as the pattern of

    (1) collective security
    (2) conflict
    (3) interventionism
    (4) balance of power
    (5) diplomatic and judicial accommodation.

179
Chapter 13

11. A foreign policy pattern designed to solve problems by direct or indirect negotiation is referred to as

(1) collective security
(2) conflict
(3) interventionism
(4) balance of power
(5) diplomatic and judicial accommodation.

12. A pattern of foreign policy by which two or more countries define and try to achieve common goals is called

(1) social, economic, and cultural cooperation
(2) diplomatic and judicial accommodation
(3) isolationism
(4) neutrality
(5) collective security.

13. A foreign policy which officially states that the country will not take sides in a particular conflict is called

(1) isolationism
(2) neutrality
(3) neutralism
(4) neutralization
(5) collective security.

14. A foreign policy resulting from a real fear of war in which the country changes "sides" frequently is called a policy of

(1) shifting allegiance
(2) neutrality
(3) balance of power
(4) neutralization
(5) collective security.

15. When the United States sends radio broadcasts to Cuba, for example, pointing out the problems in Cuba or saying the government there is corrupt, while urging the people of Cuba to revolt, this propaganda techniques would be

(1) the truth technique
(2) subversion
(3) ideological appeal
(4) the lie technique
(5) the philanthropy technique.

Chapter 13

14th Edition

16. Which one of the choices below would best describe the following scenario? The People's Republic of China and the United States conclude a trade agreement. The United States has agreed to allow China to sell anything it wants in the United States. China, on the other hand, has not agreed to allow most American products to be sold in China. China would be engaging in a tactic called

    (1) quotas
    (2) tariffing
    (3) diplomacy
    (4) subversion
    (5) zero-sum game.

Fill-in-the-Blank Questions

Write the appropriate word or words in the blanks provided.

1. The set of objectives that a country has abroad and the methods it intends to use to accomplish those objectives is referred to as

   _____.

2. One of the United States bilateral agreements involves giving China a special trade relationship with the United States. This agreement granted China _____ trading status.

3. The reduction of military budgets in the developed countries in the last couple of decades is often referred to as the _____ because such reductions freed up money to be spent elsewhere.

4. Written or oral communication between governments is referred to as

   _____.

5. The use of words, pictures, and/or actions to promote an ideology or a policy consistent with an ideology is called _____.

6. The overall goal of foreign policy is national _____.

7. The Vietnam War, because it was confined to Southeast Asia, is considered an example of _____ warfare.

8. The war between the Contras and the Nicaraguan government is considered _____ warfare because each side is being supported by either the U.S. or the former U.S.S.R.

9. The foreign policy principle that asserts that the major powers should arm themselves so heavily that no country will attack another is called the

   _____.

10. Five countries that have frequently been named as sponsors of terrorism are
_____, _____, _____, _____
and _____. *(Although previously named in this list, Iraq has been taken off the list of countries that sponsor terrorism.)*

11. A _____ treaty is an agreement between just two countries.

12. A _____ treaty is an agreement among three or more countries.

13. A very powerful military alliance that the United States founded after World War II and which the U.S. is still a part of is _____.

14. The now defunct military alliance, sponsored by the former Soviet Union, was the _____.

15. A war in which a country is not directly involved but in which some army other than its own army is used to fight the "enemy" is called _____ warfare.

16. The 17th century Dutch political theorist who is credited as the "father" of international law is _____.

17. Countries go to war for the following reasons:

    • _____
    • _____

18. According to Fredrick Hacker's analysis, members of the Islamic Jihad would be considered _____ terrorists.

19. According to Fredrick Hacker's theoretical framework, the man who shot two women in an airport because he thought they were laughing at his turban would be considered a _____ terrorist.

20. Again according to Fredrick Hacker's theory, Al Capone would be classified as a _____ terrorist.

True/False Questions

Write the correct answer in the blanks provided.

1. The World Court hears disputes among countries, and its decisions are enforced by the United Nations, by military means if necessary. _____

2. When Congress appropriates money for foreign aid, such appropriations are also considered domestic policy because tax money is being used. _____

3. Throughout history, it has been shown that, to maintain a country's physical security, a powerful military is necessary. _____

4. Trade among most countries of the world today is very much unrestricted by such things as tariffs and quotas; therefore, most countries of the world advocate free trade policies. _____

5. Terrorist groups are under the *control* of such countries as Libya, Cuba, and Iran. _____

6. The United States has pursued a policy of isolationism ever since the end of World War II. _____

7. The newest form of foreign policy that was developed in the 20th century is called collective security. _____

Discussion Questions

Use your own paper to answer the following questions.

1. What are the purposes of diplomacy? Explain by giving real or hypothetical examples of each.

2. How is economics used as a tool of foreign policy? Give specific examples along with your explanation.

3. Define international terrorism. Why would a country such as Iran use some form of terrorism as a tool of foreign policy?

4. What role do organizations such as the International Chamber of Commerce the International Red Cross play in international relations?

5. What are the specific reasons countries might engage in war? Is war ever justified? Defend your answer.

Using Your Little Gray Cells

1. What is United States policy toward the following countries: Brazil, Bulgaria, Thailand, Zimbabwe? (An excellent source for this kind of information is a State Department publication called *Background Notes on Countries of the World,* which can be found in most libraries.)

2. How successful do you think the United States was in using surrogate warfare in Nicaragua? Cite evidence for your position.

3. Assume you are the editor of the *Washington Post* newspaper. The president has just extended "most-favored-nation" trading status to communist China, which has a history of human rights violations, including incidents in which people were shot in the streets of the capital for demonstrating in favor of more freedom. Your task is to compose an editorial in which you state the paper's position on granting this most-favored-nation trading status to a country which is opposed to almost everything the United States supposedly stands for. (The essay should require some library research on your part.

To boldly go where no one has gone before!
Star Trek the Next Generation

Chapter 14

Foreign Policy: American Style

Learning Objectives

After reading and studying the chapter on foreign policy, you should have a better understanding of the following:

1. The constitutional setting of American foreign policy
2. Who and what has influence on the content of American foreign policy;
3. American foreign policy since 1789
4. Future trends of American foreign policy.

Chapter Outline

I.Constitutional grants of power
   A. Legislative authority
      1. Make laws
      2. Declare war
      3. Appropriate money
      4. Call out militia
      5. Raise and maintain armed forces
   B. Executive authority
      1. Command armed forces
      2. Negotiate treaties
      3. Appoint diplomats and cabinet members
      4. Recognize other governments
   C. Authority in area of foreign policy actually heavily weighted toward executive branch
      1. Congressional authority given to president
         a. Discretionary funds
            (1) Appropriated by Congress for president to spend for unforeseen needs in the national interest
            (2) Peace Corps
            (3) Part funding for Vietnam War
         b. Transfer of funds by president from one program to another
      2. "Black budget"
         • Only a few congressional leaders and president and some advisors know what the money is spent on
      b. Bulk spent on secret weapons

II. Inputs
   A. State Department
   B. Defense Department
   C. Socioeconomic elite
   D. Intelligence community
      1. Central Intelligence Agency
      2. National Security Agency

186

Chapter 14

3. National Reconnaissance Office
4. Department of Homeland Security
E. National Security Council
F. Public opinion
G. Interest groups
H. Mass media
I. Multinational corporations and banks
J. Non-Governmental Agencies (NGOs)
K. Congress
L. Other countries

III. An Overview of American Foreign Policy Since 1789
A. Isolationism
1. Followed or tried to follow this pattern immediately after independence from British
2. Monroe Doctrine
a. United States would not tolerate interference by Europeans in internal affairs of Western Hemisphere
b. United States interfered and colonized in Western Hemisphere
B. Neutrality
1. Followed throughout most of United States history in regard toward countries outside Western Hemisphere
2. Frequently drawn into wars for stated reasons of "morality"
C. Interventionism and collective security
1. After World War II
2. Involved all around the world
3. Major alliance: NATO
4. Truman Doctrine: military aid to those fighting communism
5. Marshall Plan: Economic aid for Western Europe
6. Nixon Doctrine: United States would provide weapons and training for "Third World" countries fighting communist takeovers
7. Reagan Doctrine
a. Continued American support for Third World countries fighting communist takeovers
b. Included active support with weapons and training for noncommunist, pro-American rebels in countries where weak leftist governments existed
D. Some current major American foreign policy directions
1. Cooperation with Russia and reduction of nuclear weapons
2. Continuation of collective security through NATO and United Nations

187

Chapter 14

3. Support for free trade
4. Continuation of "hard" line on terrorism
5. Support democratization around the world

Important Terms

"Black budget"
Arms Export Control
  Act of 1976
Attentive public
Department of
  Homeland Security
Department of State
Discretionary funds
Foreign Assistance Act
  of 1974
Interventionism
Isolationism
National security advisor
Marshall Plan
Socioeconomic elite
Intelligence Reform and
Terrorism Prevention Act

Intelligence community
Intelligence
  Authorization Act
Truman Doctrine
"Professionalization"
  of foreign policy
Monroe Doctrine
Reagan Doctrine
Senate Foreign Relations
  Committee
Neutrality
Department of Defense
NATO
The Pentagon
Marshall Plan
Non-Governmental
  Agency (NGO)

Camp David Accords
Armed Services
  Committee
NSA
National Security
  Council
NSC
CIA
Foreign Intelligence
  Surveillance Court
Nixon Doctrine
AIPAC
Shah Rezza Pahlavi
NRO
Oliver North
Multinational
  Corporation

Multiple Choice

Circle the number of the correct answer.

1. Probably the most well-known American intelligence agency is

    (1) the Central Intelligence Agency
    (2) the National Security Council
    (3) the National Security Agency
    (4) the National Reconnaissance Office
    (5) Army Intelligence.

2. The country that gets the largest share of United States security assistance is

    (1) Kuwait
    (2) Israel
    (3) Mexico
    (4) Japan
    (5) Saudi Arabia.

Chapter 14

3. "Discretionary funds" are

   (1) money Congress sets aside to use in case of a national emergency
   (2) money market certificates and mutual funds owned by the United States government for use in case of national emergency
   (3) money set aside by Congress for the president to use for unforeseen needs in the national interest
   (4) money that the president transferred from one program to another
   (5) both #3 and #4.

4. The agency charged with the coordination of intelligence gathering from all other intelligence sources is the

   (1) Central Intelligence Agency
   (2) Bureau of Intelligence and Research
   (3) National Security Agency
   (4) National Reconnaissance Office
   (5) Defense Intelligence Agency.

5. The intelligence agency that can conduct electronic surveillance within the United States and that deals with codes is

   (1) the Central Intelligence Agency
   (2) the National Security Council
   (3) the National Security Agency
   (4) the National Reconnaissance Office
   (5) Army Intelligence.

6. The intelligence agency in charge of spy satellites is

   (1) Air Force Intelligence
   (2) the National Security Council
   (3) the Defense Intelligence Agency
   (4) the National Reconnaissance Office
   (5) Army Intelligence

Chapter 14

7. Probably the most secret of all American intelligence agencies is the

   (1) Central Intelligence Agency
   (2) National Security Council
   (3) National Security Agency
   (4) National Reconnaissance Office
   (5) Defense Intelligence Agency

8. The agency that was established for the purpose of analyzing United States security and advising the president on national security matters is

   (1) the Central Intelligence Agency
   (2) the National Security Council
   (3) the National Security Agency
   (4) the National Reconnaissance Office
   (5) Army Intelligence

9. In the United States the "attentive public" for foreign policy consists of about

   (1) 5% of the country
   (2) 10% of the country
   (3) 15% of the country
   (4) 20% of the country
   (5) 25% of the country

10. IBM, ITT, GM, ARAMCO, and GE are all examples of

    (1) weapons manufacturers
    (2) companies that used to be owned primarily by Americans but that now have much of their stock owned by foreign investors
    (3) companies with substantial loans from foreign banks
    (4) United States domestic corporations
    (5) multinational corporations

11. The United States policy that placed the United States as the "protector" of North and South America from foreign intervention is referred to as the

    (1) Nixon Doctrine
    (2) Truman Doctrine
    (3) Monroe Doctrine
    (4) Marshall Plan
    (5) Reagan Doctrine

190

Chapter 14

12. The United States policy that is characterized by involvement militarily, politically, and/or economically in many places around the world is known as

(1) detente
(2) neutralism
(3) interventionism
(4) neutrality
(5) constructive engagement

13. The United States policy that included military aid to countries fighting communism was the

(1) Nixon Doctrine
(2) Truman Doctrine
(3) Monroe Doctrine
(4) Marshall Plan
(5) Reagan Doctrine

14. The United States policy that expanded the Truman Doctrine to include military assistance to countries fighting communist takeovers from internal sources was the

(1) Nixon Doctrine
(2) Anticommunist Assistance Act of 1972
(3) Monroe Doctrine
(4) Marshall Plan
(5) Reagan Doctrine

15. The policy of providing massive economic aid to Western Europe after World War II to prevent a communist takeover was the

(1) Nixon Doctrine
(2) Truman Doctrine
(3) Monroe Doctrine
(4) Marshall Plan

Chapter 14

16. The policy of active support for pro-American guerillas in places such as Nicaragua is called the

    (1) Nixon Doctrine
    (2) Truman Doctrine
    (3) Kissinger Doctrine
    (4) Rapacki Plan
    (5) Reagan Doctrine

17. The foreign policy followed by the United States government in its early years and to which it returned throughout much of its history was

    (1) Interventionism
    (2) Isolationism
    (3) Collective security
    (4) Neutrality

18. One of the following organizations is an example of an NGO. Which one?

    (1) The Red Cross
    (2) The UN World Health Organization
    (3) The American Israel Political Action Committee
    (4) The World Bank
    (5) Exxon/Mobil Corporation

Fill in the Blank

Write the appropriate word or words in the blanks provided.

1. The United States Constitution divides authority in the area of foreign policy between the _____ and _____.

2. Part of the Defense Department's budget has come to be known as the _____ because what the money is spent on is highly secret with only a few congressional leaders having any idea about its content.

3. The word that can also be used to refer to the Defense Department or the military in general but that actually is the name of the building that houses the Defense Department is the _____.

4. The _____ Court meets twice a month and grants search warrants for electronic surveillance of persons within the United States by agents of the National Security Agency.

Chapter 14

5. The Assistant for National Security Affairs, who heads the National Security Council, is usually just referred to as the

   _____.

6. The _____is a pressure group that has been very successful in influencing Congress on foreign policy matters relating to the Middle East.

7. The _____ requires the president to get the approval of Congress for all weapons sales exceeding $25 million.

8. The _____ requires the president to get the approval of Congress before any transfer of major military equipment of more than $7 million.

9. The two House and Senate committees that have more input into foreign policy matters than other committees in Congress are the _____ and _____.

10. The _____ Act of 1981 requires intelligence agencies to report to two congressional committees about their current covert activities, as well as their important upcoming operations.

11. The _____ Act created some centralization of intelligence gathering and created the position of Director of National Intelligence.

12. When the public displays very little interest in foreign policy matters and instead allows the "experts" to handle this area, the _____ of foreign policy has taken place.

13. Private organizations that have their own objectives, which might include human rights and the environmental issues, who seek to influence foreign policy are called _____.

True/False

Write the correct answer in the blanks provided.

1. Treaties can be made by the president alone, but executive agreements must have the consent of at least 2/3 of the Senate. _____

2. In reality, the president has more control over foreign policy than the Congress does. _____

Chapter 14

3. The War Powers Resolution of 1973 effectively curbed the president's ability to make war without congressional consent. _____

4. Authority in the area of foreign policy is shared equally by the executive and legislative branches of government. _____

5. The Department of State has fewer people working in it than any other executive department. _____

6. Foreign economic aid is an extremely small part of the total U.S. budget annually. _____

7. Because the various agencies, departments, and branches of the United States government are all working for the same goal in foreign policy matters, there are very few disputes regarding what policy the government should follow. _____

8. The national security advisor, because he/she heads an agency not as large as the Department of State, never have as much influence with the President as the Secretary of State. _____

9. The effects of public opinion on foreign policy in the United States are usually long term--a condition that produces very consistent American foreign policies. _____

10. Interest groups are most effective in influencing foreign policy when they get a great deal of media attention by demonstrations in Washington or elsewhere around the country. _____

Discussion Questions

1. How does foreign aid have a positive impact on the domestic economy of the United States?

2. Explain how the Defense Department and the State Department might appear to be on opposite sides of the fence in the area of foreign policy inputs to the president?

3. Define the term socioeconomic elite. Why are they generally considered to have a conservative effect on foreign policy?

Chapter 14

4. What are the characteristics of American public opinion regarding foreign policy? What explanations can be offered for the presence of these characteristics?

5. Explain the following statement: Good economic policy may not always be good political policy, whether domestic or foreign.

6. What currently is United States foreign policy in the following areas: (a) international trade, (b) terrorism, (c) collective security, (d) relations with Russia.

Using Your Little Gray Cells

1. Find out who the current Secretary of Defense, Secretary of State, and national security advisor are. What are the backgrounds of each of these individuals? Does it appear that the president relies more heavily on one of these people than on the others? (To answer this last question you will have read magazine articles concerning the president's advisors in foreign policy matters.)

2. What was the dollar value of American arms exports in a recent year? How does that compare to the estimated dollar value of Chinese weapons exports? (There are a number of sources usually in the reference section of libraries for this kind of information. One is World Military Expenditures and Arms Transfers. Ask the reference librarian for others.)

3. People tend to disagree about just what constitutes the national interest for the United States. Either in groups or by yourself, compile a list of what you think should be in the national interest of the United States, for example, promoting democratic values around the world.

Chapter 14

14th Edition

The attacks upon the Court are merely an expression of the unrest that seems to wonder vaguely whether law and order pay. When the ignorant are taught to doubt, they do not know what they safely may believe.

Oliver Wendell Holmes, Jr.
Law and the Court, 1913

Chapter 15

The Judicial Branch

Learning Objectives

After reading and studying the chapter on the judiciary in the text, you should have a better understanding of the following:

1. The meaning of the term *law*;
2. Types of law;
3. The sources of American law;
4. The adversary system of justice;
5. The jurisdiction of courts;
6. The duality of American courts;
7. State courts;
8. Federal courts;
9. Arbitration;
10. Selection of judges;
11. Judicial review
12. Judicial activism and judicial restraint.

Chapter Outline

I. Misconceptions about the Judiciary
   A. Law is unchanging
   B. Courts actively seek disputes to resolve
   C. Courts enforce/oversee policy

II. Understanding Law
   A. Law: rules made by government to regulate conduct
   B. Types of law
      1. Civil law
         a. Governs relationships between people
         b. Plaintiff: initiates lawsuit against someone
         c. Defendant: person being sued
      2. Criminal law
         a. Wrongs against the general public
         b. Felonies: serious offenses
         c. Misdemeanors: less serious offenses
   C. Origins of American law
      1. English common law
         a. Judge-made law
         b. Based on precedent--previous decisions
      2. Equity
         a. Judge-made law
         b. Can prevent actions through injunctions
      3. Statutory law
         a. Written law in the form of legislative statutes
         b. Courts determine legislative intent in deciding disputes

    c. Most common type of law
   4. Administrative law
    a. Rules from bureaucratic agencies
    b. Examples
      (1) Food and Drug Administration rules
      (2) Federal Communications Commission rules
      (3) Environmental Protection Agency rules
   5. Constitutional law
    a. Constitution is the supreme law of the land
    b. Administered through courts' power of judicial review

III. American Courts
  A. Adversary system of justice
   1. Competition between plaintiff and defendant or government and defendant
   2. Prescribed in Article III of Constitution
  B. Jurisdiction and standing
   1. Right of a court to hear and decide a case
    a. Subject matter
      (1) General jurisdiction
      (2) Special (or limited) jurisdiction
    b. Geographical jurisdiction
      (1) Cases normally heard in district where case arose
      (2) Some cases moved to another district because of undue publicity
    c. Hierarchical jurisdiction
      (1) Original jurisdiction
      (2) Appellate jurisdiction
      (3) United States Supreme Court and state supreme courts have both types
      (4) All others have one or the other
   2. Standing: substantive interest in outcome of the case in order to bring it to trial
  D. Duality of American Courts
   1. Both federal and state court systems
   2. Federal court jurisdiction
    a. Subject matter
      (1) Constitutional issue
      (2) Violations of federal law
      (3) Questions involving treaties
      (4) Matters involving admiralty and maritime law
    b. Nature of the parties
      (1) Ambassadors, public ministers, consuls
      (2) United States government
      (3) Citizens of different states

    (4) Citizens of same state claiming lands under grants from different states

    (5) State and citizen of another state

  3. Sometimes jurisdiction of federal and state courts overlaps

 E. State judicial systems

  1. Trial courts

   a. Magistrate court (justice of the peace court)

   b. Traffic court, police court, small claims court, night court, or municipal court

   c. Circuit courts

  2. Special jurisdiction courts

   a. Limited jurisdiction

   b. Probates of wills

   c. Divorces

   d. Cases involving juveniles

   e. Small claims

  3. Intermediate appellate courts: appellate jurisdiction only

  4. State supreme courts

   a. One in each state

   b. Both original and appellate jurisdictions

   c. Final court of appeals at state level

  5. Arbitration

   a. Alternative to courts

   b. Found in almost all states

  6. Selection of state judges

   a. Varies from state to state

   b. Election by voters

   c. Appointment by governor or by special commission

   d. Problems in both systems

    (1) Elected positions: party endorsement used as reward for party loyalty

    (2) Appointed positions: voters denied direct input

   e. Missouri Plan alternative

    (1) Nonpartisan commission nominates three people

    (2) Governor selects one

    (3) Continued service depends on election by voters

  7. Tenure of state judges

   a. Elected

    (1) Four to ten years

    (2) Maryland--fifteen years

   b. Appointed

    (1) Generally longer terms

    (2) Sometimes life terms

   c. Removal

    (1) Not elected for another term

    (2) Impeachment and conviction

    (3) Commission or special court review

 F. Federal Judicial Structure

1. District Court
   a. Ninety-four courts throughout the country
   b. Each state has at least one court
   c. Number of judges for each court ranges from 1 to 28
   d. Trial courts of federal judiciary
   e. Original jurisdiction only
   f. Juries for criminal trials composed of 12 members
   g. Juries for civil trials smaller--sometimes only 6
   h. Verdicts in criminal trials must be unanimous
   i. Verdicts in civil trials must have agreement of only 6
   j. Bankruptcy Court part of District Court
2. Court of Appeals (circuit courts)
   a. Eleven geographic districts (circuits)
   b. Thirteen courts
   c. Judges sit in panels of 3 to 15 members.
   d. Review decisions from lower courts and regulatory agencies
3. Supreme Court
   a. Final arbiter on Constitution, federal law, and treaties
   b. Nine judges
   c. Normally meets from October through June
   d. Hears about 200 cases for oral arguments
   e. Hears cases on Mondays, Tuesdays, Wednesdays, and sometimes Thursdays
   f. Original jurisdiction
      (1) Cases involving United States and a state
      (2) Cases between two or more states
      (3) Cases in which a state sues a citizen of another state, alien, or foreign country
   g. Appellate jurisdiction
      (1) Certification
         • Least successful method of reaching Court
         • Lower court requests technical instructions from Court
      (2) Writ of appeal
         • Questions whether state law or state constitution conflicts with federal law, treaty, or Constitution
         • Must be "substantial" constitutional question for appeal to be granted
         • Most appeals denied
      (3) Writ of certiorari
         • Most successful method of reaching Court
         • Four justices ("rule of four") must agree to hear case
      (4) Appeal to Supreme Court costly and complicated
   h. Relaxed rules for petitions filed "in the manner of a pauper" (*in forma pauperis*)
   i. Oral Arguments

            (1) In cases involving United States government, Solicitor General acts as attorney for government
            (2) Litigants (plaintiff and defendant) furnish own attorneys
            (3) Poor persons provided attorney free of charge
            (4) Written briefs (arguments) submitted by each side prior to oral argument
            (5) *Amicus curiae* briefs (interested, third-party briefs) may be submitted
    j.   Each side usually allowed one-half hour for oral arguments
    k.   Conference Friday
            (1) Private
            (2) Simple majority vote decides the case
    l.   Opinion of the Court
            (1) Assigned by Chief Justice if he/she votes in majority
            (2) Assigned by senior member in majority if Chief Justice not in majority
            (3) Opinions set precedent
            (4) Often called majority opinion
            (5) Concurring opinion possible
            (6) Dissenting opinion possible
            (7) Opinion of Court recorded in *United States Reports*

4. Special Courts
    a.   Court of Appeals for the Federal Circuit
    b.   Court of Appeals for the Armed Forces
    c.   Court of Appeals for Veterans Claims
    d.   Court of Federal Claims
    e.   Tax Court
    f.   Courts of the District of Columbia
    g.   Foreign Intelligence Surveillance Court
    h.   Court of International Trade

5. Selection of federal judges
    a.   Appointed by President with consent of Senate
    b.   Nomination
            (1) No constitutional requirements
            (2) Custom: law degree and prior judicial experience
            (3) Name of nominee sent to Senate by President
            (4) Senate Judiciary Committee hearings
            (5) Senatorial courtesy
            (6) "Politics" plays major role
            (7) Political ideology of Supreme Court nominee most important
            (8) Nominee's background
    c.   Confirmation
            (1) Simple majority vote of Senate
            (2) Senate rarely fails to approve nominee

6. Power of judiciary often underestimated
7. Judicial review

a. Power of Court to declare laws and actions of government officials unconstitutional
b. Not mentioned in Constitution
c. Granted to Court on its own through constitutional interpretation of Article VI
d. First enunciated in *Marbury v. Madison* (1803)
e. Not everyone in agreement on Court's power

8. Activism versus self-restraint
   a. Activism: judicial branch highly involved in policy making
   b. Restraint
      (1) Cases decided on merit and precedent without injecting judges' personal opinions
      (2) Constitution considered literally

9. Limitation on Court
   a. Compliance: relies on other institutions to enforce decisions
   b. Court appointments by president
   c. Congress' ability to clarify laws or introduce amendments to Constitution
   d. Public may merely ignore decision

10. Assessment of Supreme Court
    a. Court decisions often highly controversial
    b. Judiciary acts effectively particularly when
       (1) Other branches of government in agreement about an issue but are unwilling to act for political reasons
       (2) Other branches of government cannot agree on course of action

Important Terms

Adversary system of justice
Article III
Summons
Hierarchical jurisdiction
Court of Federal Claims
Duality of American courts
Court of Appeals for Veterans Claims
United States Reports
Peremptory challenges
Binding arbitration
Bench trial
Court of International Trade
Special jurisdiction courts
Territorial Court
Senate Judiciary Committee
Court of Appeals for the Federal Circuit
General jurisdiction
Memorandum of decision
Foreign Intelligence Surveillance Court
Court of Appeals for the Armed Forces
Challenges for Cause
Solicitor General
Judicial Activism
Equity
Certification
Plaintiff
Felonies

Missouri Plan
Circuit courts
Writ of Appeal
Judicial restraint
Jurisdiction
Criminal law
Judicial review
Defendant
Majority opinion
Dissenting opinion
Marbury v. Madison
District Court
Concurring opinion
Writ of certiorari
Misdemeanors
Bankruptcy Court
Tax Court
Amicus curiae brief
Tort
Precedent
Statutory law
Common law
Standing
Brief
Petit jury
Injunction

Multiple Choice Questions

Circle the number of the correct choice.

1. A set of rules enacted by government to regulate people's conduct is called

   (1) authority
   (2) law
   (3) influence
   (4) power
   (5) force.

2. One of the following crimes would probably always be a felony:

   (1) planting turnip greens all over your neighbor's front lawn
   (2) forging a check for $25
   (3) stealing a child's tricycle
   (4) burning your house down to collect the insurance money
   (5) punching your neighbor in the nose.

3. A court order that commands a person not to do something is called a (an)

    (1) writ of certiorari
    (2) writ of appeal
    (3) certification
    (4) injunction
    (5) writ of mandamus.

4. A type of law, made by judges, in which the cases are decided based on precedent is called

    (1) equity
    (2) common law
    (3) statutory law
    (4) admiralty law
    (5) administrative law.

5. A type of law, made by judges, which allows judges to prevent an action from taking place is called

    (1) equity
    (2) common law
    (3) statutory law
    (4) admiralty law
    (5) administrative law.

6. Rules and regulations issued by such agencies as the Food and Drug Administration are called

    (1) equity
    (2) common law
    (3) admiralty law
    (4) constitutional law
    (5) administrative law.

7. The type of law that grows out of the courts' use of judicial review is called

    (1) equity
    (2) common law
    (3) statutory law
    (4) constitutional law
    (5) administrative law.

8. Law that is actually written down in the form of statutes is specifically called

   (1) equity
   (2) common law
   (3) statutory law
   (4) constitutional law
   (5) none of the above.

9. American courts use an operational system known as the

   (1) checks and balance system
   (2) adversary system
   (3) brief system
   (4) equity system
   (5) administrative justice system.

10. The right of a court to hear and decide a case is known as

   (1) *stare decisis*
   (2) *jurisdiction*
   (3) *amicus curiae*
   (4) standing
   (5) injunction.

11. A type of jurisdiction that deals with the location of the court where the case is heard is called

   (1) hierarchical jurisdiction
   (2) subject matter jurisdiction
   (3) limited jurisdiction
   (4) geographical jurisdiction
   (5) general jurisdiction.

12. A type of jurisdiction referring to the level at which the case is brought to trial is called

   (1) hierarchical jurisdiction
   (2) subject matter jurisdiction
   (3) limited jurisdiction
   (4) geographical jurisdiction
   (5) general jurisdiction.

13. A court that has the right to hear and decide a case first-- before any other court-- is said to have

    (1) appellate jurisdiction
    (2) general jurisdiction
    (3) limited jurisdiction
    (4) geographical jurisdiction
    (5) original jurisdiction.

14. A court that reviews the decisions of lower courts or decisions of administrative agencies is said to have

    (1) appellate jurisdiction
    (2) general jurisdiction
    (3) limited jurisdiction
    (4) geographical jurisdiction
    (5) original jurisdiction.

15. Regarding the legal interpretation of standing, a private injury is referred to as

    (1) a crime
    (2) an injunction
    (3) a tort
    (4) a misdemeanor
    (5) a justiciable issue.

16. Regarding the legal interpretation of standing, a public injury is referred to as

    (1) a crime
    (2) an injunction
    (3) a tort
    (4) a misdemeanor
    (5) a justiciable issue.

17. Most states are phasing out their

    (1) circuit courts
    (2) special jurisdiction courts
    (3) magistrate courts
    (4) supreme courts
    (5) appellate courts.

18. The <u>minimum</u> number of jurors that can be used in a trial is set by Supreme Court ruling at

   (1) five
   (2) six
   (3) seven
   (4) eight
   (5) nine.

19. State courts that hear cases involving *major* crimes or important civil matters are often called

   (1) circuit courts
   (2) special jurisdiction courts
   (3) magistrate courts
   (4) supreme courts
   (5) appellate courts.

20. State courts that hear cases involving *minor* crimes or minor civil matters are often called

   (1) circuit courts
   (2) special jurisdiction courts
   (3) magistrate courts
   (4) supreme courts
   (5) appellate courts.

21. If a person loses a case in the state supreme court, he/she may, if the case involves a federal question, appeal to the

   (1) United States District Court
   (2) United States Court of Appeals
   (3) United States Supreme Court
   (4) Court of Appeals for the Federal Circuit
   (5) state's court of last resort.

22. If the noise of an Air Force jet breaking the sound barrier over your house broke all your windows, the court to which you would take your case to collect monetary damages would be the

   (1) Tax Court
   (2) Court of Federal Claims
   (3) Court of Appeals for the Federal Circuit
   (4) United States Supreme Court
   (5) your state supreme court.

23. If you had a patent on an invention and someone else began to manufacture your invention without your permission, the court to which you would take your case would be the

   (1) Tax Court
   (2) Court of Federal Claims
   (3) Court of Appeals for the Federal Circuit
   (4) United States Supreme Court
   (5) your state supreme court.

24. All cases involving federal crimes begin in the

   (1) state criminal courts
   (2) United States District Courts
   (3) Courts of the District of Columbia
   (4) United States Courts of Appeals
   (5) state supreme courts.

25. The United States Courts of Appeals review decisions of

   (1) the United States District Courts
   (2) federal regulatory agencies
   (3) state supreme courts
   (4) only #1 and #2
   (5) all--#1, #2, and #3.

26. The method of reaching the Supreme Court on appeal that involves a lower court's requesting technical instructions from the Supreme Court is called

   (1) a writ of appeal
   (2) a writ of certiorari
   (3) certificate
   (4) filing an amicus curiae brief
   (5) a writ of mandamus.

27. The method of reaching the Supreme Court on appeal that involves a question concerning whether a state law or state constitution conflicts with a federal law, treaty, or the national Constitution is called

   (1) a writ of appeal
   (2) a writ of certiorari
   (3) certificate
   (4) filing an amicus curiae brief
   (5) a writ of mandamus.

28. The method of reaching the Supreme Court on appeal in which the Supreme Court uses the "rule of four" is called

    (1) a writ of appeal
    (2) a writ of certiorari
    (3) certificate
    (4) filing an amicus curiae brief
    (5) a writ of mandamus.

29. The method of reaching the Supreme Court on appeal in which the Court directs the lower court to send up the record of the case for review is called

    (1) a writ of appeal
    (2) a writ of certiorari
    (3) certificate
    (4) filing an amicus curiae brief
    (5) a writ of mandamus.

30. Approval of the nominees for all federal judgeships rests with the

    (1) Senate
    (2) House of Representatives
    (3) entire Congress
    (4) Supreme Court
    (5) President.

31. When the Supreme Court merely affirms, dismisses or reverses a case it receives from a lower court without oral argument, it does so by issuing

    (1)   a writ of certiorari
    (2)   memorandum orders
    (3)   a writ of appeal
    (4)   a certification
    (5)   a brief.

Fill-in-the-Blank Questions

Write the appropriate word or words in the blanks provided.

1. The three methods by which cases may reach the Supreme Court on appeal are
    (1)   _____
    (2)   _____
    (3)   _____

2. The power of a court to declare legislative and executive actions unconstitutional ("null and void") is called _____.

3. The opinions of the Supreme Court can be found in libraries in volumes entitled the _____.

4. When a lawyer does not have a specific, legal reason for not wanting a particular juror to be seated in a trial, he/she may ask the judge to excuse that juror without giving a reason. The lawyer is said to be using one of his/her _____ challenges.

5. Crimes that are usually punishable by a fine or a short jail term are called _____.

6. The original jurisdiction of the Supreme Court of the United States is limited to cases involving

   * _____
   * _____
   * _____
   * _____

7. A trial jury is also referred to as a (an) _____ jury.

8. The jurisdiction of the federal courts is limited to cases based on _____ or the _____.

9. The classification of subject matter jurisdiction that allows a court to hear a case dealing with almost any kind of subject is called _____.

10. A person who has a substantive interest in the outcome of a case is said to have _____.

11. In terms of subject matter, the federal courts are limited to four kinds of cases:

    * _____
    * _____
    * _____
    * _____

12. _____ law deals with wrongs committed against the general public.

13. The Court used its power of judicial review for the first time in 1803 when Chief Justice John Marshall wrote the opinion in the case _____.

14. _____ law governs relationships or disputes between people.

15. In terms of the nature of the parties, the federal courts are limited to five kinds of cases:

- _____
- _____
- _____
- _____
- _____

16. The person who files a lawsuit against another person is called the _____.

17. The person who is being sued in court by another is called the _____.

18. When a defense attorney or a prosecutor wants to excuse a potential juror from service for a specific, legal reason, he/she explains the reason to the judge and the judge decides if the reason is sufficient to excuse the juror. Such requests for removal of a potential juror are called _____.

19. When an appellate court does not overturn the decision of the lower court, the appellate court is said to _____ the original decision.

20. When an appellate court overturns the decision of the lower court, the appellate court is said to _____ the original decision.

True/False Questions

Write the correct answer in the blanks provided.

1. All federal judges on the constitutional courts serve life terms ("good behavior"); whereas, the terms of state court judges are usually fixed at a certain number of years before they must stand for re-election or reappointment. _____

2. The Constitution states that federal judges must be graduates of law schools and must have had prior judicial experience. _____

3. The government cannot sue a person because civil law covers relationships or disputes between people, not between people and the government. _____

4. Modern societies have moved more and more to the use of common law rather than statutory law because of the complexity of today's world. _____

5. Federalism has produced a dual court system in the United States. _____

6. Most federal and state courts possess appellate jurisdiction. _____

7. State and federal law and treaties may not conflict with the United States Constitution. _____

8. Cases that can be heard in state courts are never heard in federal courts. _____

9. Since appeals to the Supreme Court are very costly, poor people never get their cases heard by this court. _____

10. Courts are identical from state to state. _____

11. The majority of state and federal courts possess general jurisdiction. _____

12. The federal Tax Court and the Court of Federal Claims possess general jurisdiction. _____

13. Most states today provide for binding arbitration to settle legal problems as an alternative to courts. _____

14. All Supreme Court decisions, once issued, are immediately obeyed. _____

15. Because the United States has a federal system, state judges are all selected in the same way from state to state. _____

16. All nine Supreme Court justices must vote for a case to be decided in this court. _____

17. The power of judicial review is clearly stated in Article III of the Constitution. _____

18. The power of the Supreme Court is unlimited since it alone interprets the meaning of the Constitution. _____

19. If a person wants to file for bankruptcy protection, he/she may do so *only* in a Federal District Court. _____

Discussion Questions

Use your own paper to answer the following questions.

1. A 23-year-old woman wants to have an abortion. Her mother files suit in court to try to prevent the abortion from taking place. Would the court consider the mother to have standing? Defend your answer.

2. Explain the weaknesses of both methods of selecting state judges.

3. Explain the procedure used in the United States Supreme Court: how cases reach the Supreme Court; oral arguments; briefs; conferences; voting; majority, dissenting, and concurring opinions.

4. What does the following statement mean?
   "The Supreme Court of the United States depends heavily on the willingness of the public to obey its decisions."

5. What is meant by the terms *judicial activism* and *judicial restraint?* Would a court characterized by judicial activism be considered a conservative or a liberal court generally? Give an example of a court considered judicially active and one considered judicially restrained. Which kind of court do you think is more appropriate for the United States today? Explain your answer.

6. Explain how the Supreme Court is limited in its use of power.

Using Your Little Gray Cells

1. What courts does your state have and how are the judges selected? How long are their terms of office? (If you do not know where to find this information, ask the reference librarian for assistance.)

2. Using the *United States Reports* (If you do not know how to find a case in these volumes, consult your reference librarian.), "brief" one or more of the following cases. The brief has four parts:

   (1) the issue: what is the Supreme Court being asked to decide;
   (2) the facts: what happened that lead up to the controversy;
   (3) the decision: what did the Court decide on the issue;
   (4) the reasoning: explain the reasons the Court gave for the decision.

   (a) *New York Times v. Sullivan* (1964), 376 U.S. 254
   (b) *Heffron v. International Society for Krishna Consciousness* (1981), 452 U.S. 298
   (c) *Lau v. Nichols* (1974), 414 U.S. 563.

3. Who are the current Supreme Court justices? Report on the background of each including their age when appointed, year of appointment, which president appointed them, education, prior judicial experience, experience other than judicial, religion, race, sex, and ideology.

4. Justice Clarence Thomas faced stiff opposition to his appointment to the Supreme Court. Write an essay in which you present the background of the nomination and confirmation and then present your argument in favor of or against Justice Thomas' confirmation.

5. Explain what you think Oliver Wendell Holmes, Jr. meant by the quote on the first page of this chapter of the study guide.

Chapter 16

Citizens and the Law:
The Rights of the Accused

Learning objectives

After reading and studying the chapter on citizens and the law, you should have a better understanding of the following:

1. What constitutes reasonable searches and seizures;
2. Probable cause;
3. The exclusionary rule;
4. Procedures used by police when placing someone under arrest;
5. The right to remain silent;
6. The right to an attorney;
7. Impoundment of personal property;
8. Booking a suspect and interrogation procedures;
9. Police lineups for identification purposes;
10. The purposes of and procedures used for bond hearings, preliminary hearings and arraignments;
11. The right to a speedy trial;
12. Trial procedures;
13. The defendant's rights during a trial.

Chapter Outline

I. The Pre-Trial Phase of Criminal Procedure
  A. Stop and search
    1. Police may stop and/or frisk individual if they have probable cause to believe he/she has committed crime or is about to commit crime (*Terry v. Ohio,* 1968)
    2. "Evidence" obtained in search without probable cause inadmissible in court: exclusionary rule
    3. Plain view rule
    4. With probable cause, police may search open areas of car within suspect's immediate control
      a. Normally closed areas, whether locked or not, cannot be searched without search warrant
      b. These areas considered part of "expectation of privacy"
    4. Searches without warrants
      a. Searches of closed areas which were opened by suspect
      b. Can be made under "exigent circumstances" which usually must be confirmed by
        (1) Police surveillance
        (2) Videotapes

  c. Examples
    (1) Searches of moveable scenes of crime
    (2) Searches by border patrol
    (3) Searches by airport guards
    (4) Searches by prison guards
    (5) Searches of fields for marijuana
B. Arrest
 1. Made with probable cause to suspect person has committed crime
 2. Reading suspect's rights (*Miranda v. Arizona*, 1966)
  a. Right to remain silent
  b. Anything you say may be used against you
  c. Right to presence of attorney
  d. If you cannot afford one, attorney will be appointed for you
C. Impoundment and inventory of personal property
 1. Any evidence found can be used against suspect
 2. Police do not have right to tear cars apart without warrant
D. Booking
 1. Procedure varies with size of police department
 2. Information gathered
  a. Name
  b. Place of residence
  c. Age
  d. Sex
  e. Race
  f. Details of arrest
  g Past criminal record
 3. Suspect does have right to remain silent and right to attorney at this stage
 4. Right to phone call, but must be requested
 5. Fingerprinting and photographing of suspect
 6. Removal and inventorying of personal effects
 7. Suspect placed in holding cell while officer checks fingerprints and prior criminal record and discusses case with prosecutor
E. Further interrogation
 1. If charge is misdemeanor, suspect may post bail immediately, have possessions returned, receive date for court appearance, and leave
 2. Otherwise, more questions
  a. Police cannot pump stomach to obtain evidence
  b. Police can take x-rays and blood tests under certain circumstances
  c. Police cannot force suspect to take lie detector test
  d. Suspect has right to stop talking and have attorney any time

F. Lineup for identification purposes
    1. Suspect must submit to lineup
    2. Rights of suspect
        a. Presence of attorney at lineup where witnesses are present
        b. Presence of attorney free of charge if suspect cannot afford attorney's fees
        c. Suspect must be informed that he/she and others in lineup will have to repeat certain words or phrases; suspect cannot refuse
G. Plea bargaining
    1. Agreements between defendant and his/her attorney and prosecutor to plead guilty to lesser charge
    2. Frequent in criminal justice system
    3. Not always obtained
H. Bond hearing
    1. Must occur within 24 hours of arrest
    2. Writ of habeas corpus: court order to police which requires them to bring person to court
    3. Purposes
        a. To inform person of charges
        b. To establish bail (if any)
            (1) Person considered innocent till proven guilty
            (2) Eighth Amendment prohibits "excessive" bail
            (3) Can be denied
                • Those accused of capital crimes
                • Those who demonstrated past unreliability
                • Those who pose threat to public
            (4) Types of bonds (bail)
                • Individual recognizance bond
                • Deposit bond
                • Cash bond
I. Further search and seizure
    1. Searches of houses without warrant
        a. With permission of owner or someone who lives with suspect, subject to certain qualifications
        b. If police in "hot pursuit"
        c. If police see crime being committed in house
        d. If police believe someone's life is in danger
    2. Warrants obtained in court
        a. Require probable cause
            (1) Suspicion alone not sufficient
            (2) "Fishing expeditions" prohibited
        b. Describe place to be searched and persons or things to be seized

14th edition

    c. With valid search warrant, any contraband may be seized and used in court whether listed on warrant or not

   3. Wiretaps require search warrants

  J. Preliminary hearing

   1. Constitution requires grand jury indictment for federal crimes

   2. States use preliminary hearings

   3. Used to determine if evidence sufficient to hold trial

  K. Arraignment

   1. Usually 4 to 6 weeks after preliminary hearing

   2. Purpose to bring defendant to court to answer charges

   3. If guilty plea, judge sets sentencing date

   4. If not-guilty plea, judge sets trial date

   5. Defendant's rights

    a. Trial by impartial jury

     (1) Federal juries require 12 people and unanimous vote to convict

     (2) State juries require minimum of 6 people and simple majority to convict

    b. Trial usually held in locale where crime alleged

    c. Change of venue

     (1) Trial moved to another place

     (2) Or jury brought in from another area

     (3) Results from undue publicity

     (4) Or defendant disliked in local community

    d. Can waive right to jury trial and opt for bench trial

    e. Speedy trial (6th Amendment)

     (1) Supreme Court refused to define "speedy"

     (2) Speedy Trial Act, 1974

      • Applies to federal courts only

      • If defendant not tried within 60 days of arrest, charges must be dropped

     (3) State courts: usually 120 to 180 days from time of arrest

II. Trial Phase of Criminal Procedure

  A. Pre-trial counsel

   1. Right to be represented by attorney (6th Amendment)

   2. Right to remain silent (5th Amendment)

    a. Not required to take stand in own defense

    b. If defendant takes stand, prosecutor has right to cross examine

   3. Right to be confronted by witnesses (sixth Amendment)

   4. Right to subpoena witnesses on defendant's behalf

Chapter 16

B. Trial
1. Adversary system of justice: defendant against government
2. Both sides present opening statements usually
3. Both sides present witnesses and cross examine each other's witnesses
4. Either side may object to admission of evidence or statements made by witnesses, prosecutor, or defense attorney
    a. Judge may overrule objection and allow testimony or evidence
    b. Judge may sustain objection and disallow testimony or evidence
C. Post-trial counsel
1. Defendant advised he/she couldn't be tried again for same offense
    a. Violates double-jeopardy rule in 5th Amendment
    b. If same incident involves state and federal crime, both governments may try person
    c. Person, if found innocent, may not sue government to recover court costs, attorney fees, etc., unless arrest deemed false arrest, i.e., with malice

III. Postscript
A. Criminal procedure still lacks definitive clarity
B. Reaffirmation of *Miranda* rules
C. Use of thermal imaging device requires a warrant
D. Detention of suspect outside home while police get a warrant constitutional
E. Evidence found in car on pretext of traffic stop can be used.

Important Terms

Gideon v. Wainwright, 1963	Public defender	Search warrant
Impoundment of property	Probable cause	Stop and frisk
Inevitable discovery rule	Eighth Amendment	Arraignment
Preliminary hearing	Contraband	Indictment
Expectation of privacy	Bench trial	Direct examination
Speedy Trial Act, 1974	Lein check	Change of venue
Cross examination	Fifth Amendment	True bill
Miranda v. Arizona, 1966	Exclusionary rule	Bail
Independent source doctrine	Good faith rule	No bill
Adversary system of justice	Sixth Amendment	Booking
Fourth Amendment	Line-up	Subpoena
Constitutional technicality	Plea bargain	Pat down
Writ of *habeas corpus*	Double jeopardy	Show-up

14th edition

Multiple Choice Questions

Circle the number of the correct answer.

1. The constitutional amendment which deals with searches and seizures is the

    (1) Fourth Amendment
    (2) Fifth Amendment
    (3) Sixth Amendment
    (4) Eighth Amendment
    (5) Tenth Amendment.

2. The constitutional amendment which deals with the right to a speedy trial is the

    (1) Fourth Amendment
    (2) Fifth Amendment
    (3) Sixth Amendment
    (4) Eighth Amendment
    (5) Tenth Amendment.

3. The constitutional amendment which deals with the right to remain silent is the

    (1) Fourth Amendment
    (2) Fifth Amendment
    (3) Sixth Amendment
    (4) Eighth Amendment
    (5) Tenth Amendment.

4. The constitutional amendment which deals with excessive bails is the

    (1) Fourth Amendment
    (2) Fifth Amendment
    (3) Sixth Amendment
    (4) Eighth Amendment
    (5) Tenth Amendment.

(Refer to the footnotes in the chapter to answer questions 5 through 10.)

5. The Supreme Court case in which the Court ruled that an indigent defendant must be provided with an attorney at no charge was

    (1) Miranda v. Arizona
    (2) Gideon v. Wainwright
    (3) Rochin v. California
    (4) United States v. Wade
    (5) Terry v. Ohio.

6. The Supreme Court case in which the Court ruled a person under arrest had to be told his/her "rights" was

    (1) Miranda v. Arizona
    (2) Gilbert v. California
    (3) Rochin v. California
    (4) South Dakota v. Neville
    (5) Gideon v. Wainwright.

7. The Supreme Court case in which the Court ruled that police could not pump a person's stomach to obtain evidence was

    (1) Miranda v. Arizona
    (2) Gilbert v. California
    (3) Rochin v. California
    (4) South Dakota v. Neville
    (5) Gideon v. Wainwright.

8. The Supreme Court case in which the Court ruled x-rays and blood tests could be used by police on a suspect even against his/her will under certain circumstances was

    (1) Miranda v. Arizona
    (2) Gilbert v. California
    (3) Schmerber v. California
    (4) South Dakota v. Neville
    (5) Gideon v. Wainwright.

14th edition

9. The Supreme Court case in which the Court ruled that a person had to be told his/her "rights" before being placed in a police lineup was

    (1) Miranda v. Arizona
    (2) Gideon v. Wainwright
    (3) Rochin v. California
    (4) United States v. Wade
    (5) Terry v. Ohio.

10. The Supreme Court case in which the Court ruled that "stop and frisk" procedures used by police were constitutional where there is reasonable suspicion that the person has committed or is about to commit a crime was

    (1) Miranda v. Arizona
    (2) Gideon v. Wainwright
    (3) Rochin v. California
    (4) United States v. Wade
    (5) Terry v. Ohio.

11. In a trial, the defendant's attorney

    (1) May take notes when a prosecution witness is testifying but may not question the witness directly.
    (2) May interrupt the prosecutor's direct examination to refute what the witness is saying.
    (3) May cross examine the prosecution witness when the direct examination is concluded.
    (4) Must put the defendant on the stand immediately after the direct examination so that the defendant can refute what the witness has said.
    (5) Must ask for a recess so that he/she go outside to request an ambulance for the heart attack the attorney is about to have because of the witness's testimony.

12. The constitutional amendment which requires that persons accused of federal crimes be indicted by a grand jury is the

    (1) Fourth Amendment
    (2) Fifth Amendment
    (3) Sixth Amendment
    (4) Eighth Amendment
    (5) Tenth Amendment.

14th edition

13. A court procedure in which the defendant must answer the charges against him/her, usually by entering a "guilty" or "not guilty" plea is called

    (1) an indictment
    (2) an arraignment
    (3) a preliminary hearing
    (4) a trial
    (5) pre-trial counsel.

14. Juries at the federal level must be composed of

    (1) six jurors
    (2) seven jurors
    (3) nine jurors
    (4) twelve jurors
    (5) sixteen jurors.

15. Juries at the state level must have a minimum of

    (1) six jurors
    (2) seven jurors
    (3) nine jurors
    (4) twelve jurors
    (5) sixteen jurors.

16. The Speedy Trial Act of 1974 demands that a defendant in a federal court be brought to trial within

    (1) 60 days of arrest
    (2) 60 to 120 days of arrest
    (3) 120 days of arrest
    (4) 180 days of arrest
    (5) 120 to 180 days of arrest.

17. Most states will bring a defendant to trial within

    (1) 60 days of arrest
    (2) 60 to 120 days of arrest
    (3) 120 days of arrest
    (4) 180 days of arrest
    (5) 120 to 180 days of arrest.

18. A court order which demands the appearance of witnesses at a trial is called a (an)

    (1) writ of habeas corpus
    (2) subpoena
    (3) indictment
    (4) arraignment
    (5) writ of certiorari.

19. A court order that requires police to bring a suspect they are holding before a court to show cause why that suspect should not be released is called a (an)

    (1) writ of mandamus
    (2) arraignment
    (3) writ of certiorari
    (4) writ of habeas corpus
    (5) preliminary hearing.

Fill-in-the-Blank Questions

Write the appropriate word or words in the blanks provided.

1. When an attorney objects to the admission of some testimony in court and the judge agrees with the attorney and rules that the testimony is inadmissible, the objection is said to have been _____.

2. When an attorney objects to the admission of some testimony in court and the judge disagrees with the attorney and rules that the testimony is admissible, the objection is said to have been _____.

3. Being tried twice for the same crime is referred to as _____.

4. A change of _____ refers to a change in the location of a trial, probably as a result of undue publicity.

5. To obtain a search warrant or to arrest someone, police must have _____, which means they have reason to believe the suspect has committed a crime .

6. _____ refers to agreements made between the defendant and his/her attorney and the prosecutor so that the defendant can plead guilty to a lesser charge, thereby avoiding a trial and possibly more severe punishment.

14th edition

7. The _____ is used by the courts to throw out evidence that was obtained by police illegally.

8. The so-called *Miranda* rights are

   (1) _____
   (2) _____
   (3) _____
   (4) _____

9. The first stage of police procedure after a suspect reaches the police station, which involves gathering general information about the suspect, fingerprinting, etc., is referred to as _____.

10. The term _____ refers to any illegal item or items a person may have in his possession.

11. The court will appoint a (an) _____ to act as attorney for an indigent defendant.

12. A suspect's rights, which must be told to him/her if he/she is to be placed in a police line-up, include

    a. _____
    b. _____
    c. _____

13. Under what circumstances may police search a house without a warrant?

    a. _____
    b. _____
    c. _____
    d. _____

14. A (An) _____ of indictment is a statement issued by a grand jury in which the grand jury asserts that there is sufficient evidence to charge a person with a crime.

15. A (An) _____ trial refers to a trial by a judge without a jury.

16. States utilize _____ to determine if there is sufficient evidence to hold a person for trial.

17. The _____ allows the use of evidence obtained under a warrant police believed to be legal but later proved invalid.

14th edition

18. The _____ applies if police obtained evidence illegally but can prove that it would have been discovered eventually without a search warrant.

19. Sometimes called the retroactive probable cause rule, the _____ doctrine allows prosecutors to use evidence traceable to illegal police or governmental activity if the evidence has a lawful independent source.

20. When the police stop someone, they may do a _____, in which they receive information via their radios or computers about you, such as if there are any outstanding warrants with your name on them.

21. Questioning of a prosecution witness by the prosecutor would be referred to as _____ examination.

22. Questioning of a prosecution witness by the defense attorney would be referred to as _____ examination.

23. Questioning of a defense witness by the defense attorney would be referred to as _____ examination.

24. Questioning of a defense witness by the prosecutor would be referred to as _____ examination.

25. When someone is placed on trial in the United States, there is supposed to be a _____ of innocence.

True/False Questions

Write the correct answer in the blanks provided.

1. Police may visually scan a car without a search warrant if the driver has been stopped for a legitimate reason. _____

2. Impounding a vehicle has been ruled unconstitutional by the Supreme Court as a violation of the Fourth Amendment's search and seizure provisions. _____

3. Anything that police find while inventorying a suspect's possessions is not admissible as evidence in court unless it pertains to the reason the person was arrested. _____

4. Guilty verdicts by all juries, whether federal or state, must be unanimous. _____

14th edition

5. A person accused of a felony has the right to a trial by jury but may waive this right if he/she so desires. _____

6. The Supreme Court has defined a "speedy" trial as one which begins within 60 to 180 days after the defendant has been arrested. _____

7. Police may not search a house or a person without a search warrant because persons and houses are considered inviolable. _____

8. Usually police may not search locked or closed areas of a car without a search warrant. _____

9. The Eighth Amendment guarantees the right to bail. _____

10. If a person robs a bank (Bank robbery is both a state and a federal crime.), the robber could only be tried by one or the other government, not both, since to try the person in both federal and state courts would be double jeopardy. _____

11. Police may search a house without a warrant if they see someone commit a crime in the house. _____

12. If a suspect agrees to take a lie detector test and the results indicate that he/she is lying, these results can be used as evidence in his/her trial. _____

13. If a person has been arrested by police with a search warrant issued with probable cause, is tried but found innocent, then the person can sue the government to collect his/her lost wages and attorney's fees. _____

14. The Supreme Court has ruled that the right to indictment by a grand jury does not apply to states. _____

15. The prosecuting attorney can cross examine any witness except the defendant, even if the defendant chooses to take the stand, because to cross examine the defendant would violate the ban against self-incrimination. _____

16. If someone who lives in your apartment with you allows the police to enter the premises without your permission to search your room, anything the police obtain in their search could not be used as evidence against you in court because you yourself did not give them permission. _____

17. If a search warrant specifies that the police are looking for drugs at your house. They open desk drawer and find evidence of bookmaking (taking bets), such evidence could not be used against you in court. _____

14th edition

18. Wiretapping is considered unconstitutional under any circumstances as an invasion of privacy. _____

19. Police may search fields for marijuana unless there are no-trespassing signs posted. _____

20. Prison guards and border guards do not need search warrants to conduct searches in the prison or at border crossings, respectively. _____

21. As long as the police do not physically enter your house or place of business, they do not need search warrants to use equipment that essentially sees though the building or equipment that allows them to hear what is being said in a house or building. _____

22. In the United States, the defendant must prove his/her innocence beyond a reasonable doubt. _____

23. According to the doctrine about expectation of privacy, suspects would have no expectation of privacy while they were seated in the back seat of a police car. _____

24. Police must obtain a search warrant if they wish to use thermal imaging devices. _____

25. Evidence obtained by police who searched a car on the pretext of making a general traffic stop who really wanted to search for drugs cannot be used in court against the defendants. _____

26. Police can *Mirandize* a suspect at any point in their interrogation. _____

27. There are some circumstances where police may search closed areas in a car or closed items within the car without a warrant. _____

Discussion Questions

Use your own paper to answer the following questions.

1. Explain the meaning of the term *adversary system of justice.*

2. Often times the exclusionary rule has been referred to as a constitutional technicality. Explain the meaning of the term *constitutional technicality.* Do you believe the exclusionary rule is such a technicality? Explain your answer.

3. Do you agree or disagree with the final statement in this chapter: "In this era of high crime, coupled with terrorist activity, security may win out over liberty. Defend your answer.

Using Your Little Gray Cells

1. (I am indebted to my colleague Lyn Rosenburg for many of the ideas contained in the exercises in this question, as well as #2. **Search and Seizure Exercises**: decide in each of the following situations if the search is legal and whether or not the evidence could be used against the individual in court. <u>Give reasons for your answers.</u> Write your answers in the space provided.

   a. Tooky's former boyfriend breaks into her apartment and looks around for pictures or letters indicating a new boyfriend. Instead of evidence of a new, "significant other," he finds drugs, which he turns over to the police.

   b. Stella's former boyfriend walks into her apartment after finding the door unlocked and looks around for pictures or letters indicating a new boyfriend. Instead of evidence of a new, "significant other," he finds drugs, which he turns over to the police.

   c. Buford checks out of a hotel. The police arrive and ask the maid to turn over the contents of the wastebasket from Buford's room. They find evidence that Buford is planning a robbery.

   d. The police see "Pig", a known drug dealer, standing on a corner on a downtown street. They stop and search "Pig" and find drugs in his pocket.

14th edition

e. Geraldine is observed shoplifting items in a store. Police chase Geraldine into her apartment building and arrest her <u>outside</u> the door of her apartment. The apartment door is unlocked; they enter, search it, and find a large amount of stolen goods.

f. The police suspect "Dog" of receiving stolen goods. They go to his house where "Moose", "Dog's" roommate, agrees to let them search the house. The police find stolen items in Dog's closet.

g. Esmerelda is arrested for reckless driving. Then the police search her purse and find a pistol for which she has no permit.

h. The police receive a tip from a reliable informant that Earl has counterfeit money in his office. Acting on this information, they get a search warrant. However, instead of counterfeit money the police find illegal drugs where the informant said the counterfeit would be.

i. Elmer Gluson is driving down the road with a broken tail light on his car. A police officer follows Elmer and attempts to pull Elmer over by turning on his flashers and using his siren. Elmer is oblivious to the officer because of the music blaring from his car stereo which is loud enough to wake the dead! Finally Elmer sees the officer's signals and pulls over. The officer asks Elmer to get out of the car for a pat down search during which the officer finds a .38 police special taped to Elmer's leg. Is the pat-down search legal? Can the police use the gun as evidence against Elmer in a trial?

14th edition

j. Officers Daisy Turnipseed and Sylvia Tweedy witness a suspect breaking a car window and stealing the airbag. The suspect runs down the street and the police follow him. the "perp" then runs into a house and refuses to admit Turnipseed and Tweedy claiming that they need a search warrant to enter and/or search the premises. Is the suspect correct? Explain.

k. Officer Tom Toms is walking his beat at about 9:00 p.m. He hears a loud argument coming from one of the houses. He stops in front of the house. Through an open front door, he sees a woman just beating this man "up one side and down the other" in the front room of the house. The woman finally picks up an encyclopedia and conks the man on the head. Officer Toms enters the house and arrests the woman, who is identified as Gloxinia Recker. Her husband, Carson Recker, is apparently all right, although still seeing stars, and keeps telling Tom that he doesn't want to press charges. After cuffing Gloxinia and reading her rights, Tom sees on the coffee table some white power which Tom thinks is cocaine. He then cuffs Carson and reads him his rights also. Gloxinia is charged with assault and battery, and both Gloxinia and Carson Recker are charged with possession of a controlled substance. The couple's attorney claims that Officer Toms had no right to enter the house and that anything seized without a search warrant cannot be used against the Reckers in court. Is the attorney correct?

l. Officers Lilly Lively and Rip Torn obtain a warrant to search a house and a detached garage at 616 Battle Street for illegal weapons. They do not find the contraband they are looking for so they decide to search an automobile parked in the driveway. Luckily for Lilly and Rip, they find a bag of betting slips (evidence of illegal gambling) under the front seat of the car. What is the status of these betting slips as evidence?

m. Officers Powers Haus and Greenwich "Green" Means get a search warrant for a used car dealership at 802 Recker Road. They have had this place staked out for some time on a tip that the dealership was actually a "chop shop." They execute the warrant and, sure enough, they find the evidence they are seeking. The owners and several "mechanics" are arrested. At the trial their defense attorneys claim the evidence cannot be used against their clients in court because it was obtained in an illegal search and seizure; namely, that the search warrant had 208 Recker Road as the place to be searched instead of the correct address of 802 Recker Road. Are the defense attorneys correct?

n. The police stop a "Beamer" because the driver, Reginald Twitwater, was driving erratically all over the road. They ask "Reggie" to get out of the car. He does, still smoking his marijuana. They placed him under arrest, searched him and found cocaine in his pocket. They then asked his passenger, Binky Whitherspoon, to get out of the car also. They searched Binky and a shopping bag he had with him that he said was full of things he had purchased at Sears. The police found cocaine in the Sears bag also and arrested Binky. Were these two searches legal? Why or why not? Would the police be justified in asking for a search warrant for the local Sears store? Why or why not?

14th edition

2. **Rights of the Accused Scenarios:** Answer the questions based on these scenarios in the spaces provided.

a. Susie Que is arrested and charged with fraud, to wit, a real estate scam. She is informed of her rights and refuses an attorney saying that she wants to "spill her guts." Ms. Que reveals all about the workings of the scam and not only incriminates herself but also her accomplices, Freddie "The Foot" Cardigan and Carl "The Cat" Gato. When Susie Que comes to trial, her attorney argues that anything she said to the police cannot be used against her in court because she made the statements without the presence of an attorney which violates her rights under the Fifth Amendment. Is Que's attorney correct? Explain.

b. Brutus Beagle is arrested and charged with assaulting Homer "The Hiccup" Coleman. Brutus is taken to the police station, is informed of his rights again, but decides he doesn't want a lawyer during questioning. He signs a statement that he is answering questions without the presence of an attorney voluntarily and without any promises made by the police. Brutus answers a couple of questions put to him by the police during custodial interrogation but then changes his mind and says he wants a lawyer. The police tell him he cannot have one since he signed the waiver of his right to an attorney. Are the police correct?

14th edition

c. Natasha Nietzsche is arrested for burglary. Her attorney arrives and advises her to take the lie detector test that the police asked Natasha to take. Since she contends that she is innocent, the attorney believes she will pass the test and the police will look elsewhere for their suspect. Natasha takes the test, but the results indicate that she is probably lying. At her trial the prosecutor tries to introduce the results of the lie detector test, but the defense attorney objects, urging the judge to use the Exclusionary Rule to bar the "evidence." What should the judge do? Exclude or admit the test results? Why?

d. "Spicy Bits," the stage name of an exotic dancer whose real name is Mildred Ethelrod, is arrested and charged with murdering the owner of the night club where she works. Spicy has never been arrested before and doesn't have a lot of money with which she could flee the jurisdiction of the court, i.e., "take a powder." At her arraignment she pleads not guilty and her attorney asks that she be released on $50,000 bail. The prosecutor objects to bail and urges the judge to deny bail for Spicy since the crime is murder. Spicy's attorney says that the Eighth Amendment guarantees the right to bail. Who is correct: the defense or the prosecution? Explain.

3.   Read the following and discuss in groups or with a partner the questions at the end of the paragraph.

McCleskey v. Kemp, 481 U.S. 278 (1987)

An African American named Warren McCleskey was convicted and sentenced to death in Georgia for the murder of a police officer during the commission of an armed robbery. On appeal to the Supreme Court, McCleskey's attorney argued that in Georgia, as well as nationally, blacks who kill whites are four times more likely to be sentenced to death than people who kill blacks. As a result, he argued, the death penalty was being applied in a racially discriminatory manner and, therefore, violated the Fourteenth Amendment's clause on "equal protection of the laws" and the Eighth Amendment's ban on "cruel and unusual punishment." He urged the Court to overturn McCleskey's conviction on that basis.

- If you had been on the Supreme Court, would you have agreed with the attorney's argument and overturned McCleskey's conviction based on the statistical evidence presented?

- If you accept McCleskey's claim of racial discrimination, could a case also be made of sex discrimination since the overwhelming majority of persons sentenced to death are also males?

The very aim and end of our institutions is just this: that we may think what we like and say what we think.

Oliver Wendell Holmes, 1860

It has been observed that those who clamour most loudly for liberty do not most liberally grant it.

John Milton, 1779

When the press is free and every man able to read, all is safe.
Thomas Jefferson, 1816

Chapter 17
Civil Liberties: Freedom in America

Learning Objectives

After reading and studying the chapter on civil liberties, you should have a better understanding of the following:

1. The meaning of religious freedom in the United States and the Supreme Court's interpretations of the doctrine of separation of church and state;
2. The limitations on and controversies surrounding freedom of speech and freedom of the press;
3. The meaning of "cruel and unusual punishment;"
4. The ownership of firearms;
5. The right of eminent domain;
6. The right to assemble peacefully;
7. Government regulation of sexual practices;
8. The legal status of suicide;
9. Other rights retained by the people.

Chapter Outline

I. Freedom of Religion
  A. Establishment Clause
    1. Religion in public schools
      a. Schools may not sponsor or encourage prayer
      b. Prayer not prohibited on individual basis
      c. School-sponsored, official prayer in public schools violates establishment clause of First Amendment
    2. Other rulings
      a. School-sponsored *Bible* reading and recitation of the *Lord's Prayer* prohibited
      b. Allows student-led prayer at graduation
      c. Public schools must allow religious groups to use school facilities after hours if schools allow other community groups to use facilities
      d. Posting of religious materials by themselves prohibited
      e. No prayer at sporting events, even student-led prayers
    3. Religious subjects and subjects with religious implications
      a. Classes allowed as part of regular curriculum
        (1) The *Bible* as literature
        (2) Comparative religion
      b. Cannot prohibit teaching of evolution merely because of negative religious implications
      c. Religion instructors not allowed to teach religion classes even on voluntary basis on school days

4. Prayers in Congress and state legislatures
   a. Supreme Court ruled these constitutional
   b. Adults not "susceptible to religious indoctrination or peer pressure"
5. Aid to parochial and private elementary and secondary schools
   a. Child benefit theory
      ▪ Tax money can be used if assistance benefits child rather than school
   b. Examples
      • Transporting parochial-school students to and from school
      • Purchasing secular textbooks
      • Providing lunch programs
      • Providing tests for speech and hearing problems
      • Reimbursing cost of scoring state-required tests
      • Public-school teachers may teach remedial   subjects in parochial schools.
   c. States may allow state income tax deduction for parents of nonpublic-school children
6. Prohibited aid
   a. Salaries of teachers (except remedial subjects)
   b. Equipment
   c. Counseling for students
   d. Preparation of teachers' tests
   e. Repair of school facilities
   f. Transportation of students to and from field trips
   g. Teaching by public-school teachers, except for remedial subjects
7. Secondary schools receiving any federal funds must allow religious clubs and others a place to meet if other community groups are allowed to meet on school grounds.
8. Aid to parochial and private colleges and universities
   a. Considerably more relaxed rules
   b. Tax money may be used for
      ▪ Construction of buildings not used for religious purposes
      ▪ Secular educational programs
   c. Rationale: college students less susceptible to religious indoctrination and peer pressure
9. Religious displays on public property
   a. Allowed or disallowed on case-by-case basis
   b. Display of nativity scene on public property allowed if
   c. Motivation was celebration of national holiday
   d. Intention commercial, not religious
   e. No excessive entanglement between government and religious groups

B. Free Exercise Clause
  1. Prohibited
     a. Snake handling
     b. Use of mind-altering drugs
     c. Polygamy
     d. Parental refusal of medical treatment for children in life-threatening cases
     e. Parental refusal of vaccinations for children
  2. Allowed
     a. Jehovah's Witnesses not required to salute American flag
     b. Amish parents not required to send children to public school beyond 8th grade
  3. Many religious practices protection now in jeopardy because of recent Court ruling
     a. State no longer required to show a "compelling state interest"
     b. State may now prohibit certain religious practices as long as the law is content neutral--not directed at any particular religious group
  4. Employees cannot be fired because of refusal to work Saturdays or Sundays (for religious reasons)
  5. Court upheld a state's refusal to grant unemployment benefits to those who were fired from their jobs for using peyote, even though its use may have been for religious purposes.
  6. However, Court also ruled a religious group could use a tea with a hallucinogen during its ceremony.

II. Freedom of Speech and Press
  A. Not absolute rights
  B. Preferred Position Doctrine
     1. Freedom of speech and press should get highest priority
     2. Almost advocates no censorship
     3. Court still uses this doctrine in cases with political overtones
  C. Direct incitement
     1. Communication may be prohibited if it advocates imminent, illegal action.
     2. Judgment call by police on the scene
  D.. Prior restraint
     1. Prevention of publication or speech viewed harmful by government
     2. Generally not acceptable to Supreme Court
     2. Exceptions fall into category of military and national security matters
  E. Least drastic means
     1. Purpose of law restricting speech or press first deemed constitutional

      2.   Then, Court determines if method used to restrict speech or press is least drastic way of doing it

F.   Content neutral
    1.   Regulating activity rather than content of activity
    2.   Example
        a.   Law could prohibit distribution of handbills at intersection
        b.   Law could not prohibit distribution of just political handbills at intersection

G.   Centrality of political speech
    1.   Political speech particularly important to Court
    2.   Right to criticize government essential to maintain freedom
    3.   Example
        a.   Calling your neighbor a thief may be deemed unlawful
        b.   But calling president a thief constitutionally protected
    4.   Patriot Act

D.   Libel and slander
    1.   Written and oral statements defaming another person
    2.   Not protected speech or press
    3.   Actionable (suing for damages) only if observed by third party
    4.   Suits for libel or slander by public officials or public figures difficult
        a.   Must prove statement untrue
        b.   Must prove statement made with actual malice

E.   "Swearing" in public
    1.   Generally permissible
    2.   May be prohibited if
        a.   Directed at someone and might produce violence
        b.   Loud and disturbing to peace

F.   Symbolic speech
    1.   Gestures considered speech
    2.   May be prohibited if directed at someone and might provoke violence
    3.   Political symbolic speech
    4.   Allowed
        a.   Wearing armbands in schools allowed under some circumstances
        b.   Burning American flag
    5.   Not allowed
        a.   Burning draft card
        b.   Prohibited under Selective Service Act

G.   Minors treated differently
    1.   Searches in schools
    2.   Mandatory drug tests for athletes
    3.   Curfews

H.   Regulation of the Internet

1. Communications Decency Act ruled unconstitutional
2. Child Internet Protection Act, 1998
   a. Court upheld portions of action in 2003 that denied funds to libraries that did not use filtering/blocking software for porn
   b. 2008, Court ruled some nude photos of children (i.e., newborns) not pornographic
3. Communication that threatens must meet "true threat" standard
4. ISPs can restrict what goes to their subscribers
5. Students may post sites critical of their school even if vulgar language used

I. Posting of advertisements
   1. May be regulated if law is content neutral
   2. Applies to sound trucks also

J. Regulation of sale of sexually explicit material
   1. Obscenity not protected speech
      a. Attempted to define obscenity
         (1) Material dealing "with sex in a manner appealing to prurient interest"
         (2) Considered obscene if the average person, applying "contemporary community standards," would be offended
         (3) Excluded artistic, literary, and scientific material
      b. Confusion resulted in application of definition
      c. Attempted to clarify test for obscenity
      d. Guidelines: essentially left issue to local community
         (1) Would average person, applying "contemporary community standards" find material in its entirety appealing to prurient interest
         (2) Does work describe, in patently offensive way, sexual conduct specifically defined by applicable state law
         (3) Does work in its entirety lack serious literary, artistic, political, or scientific value
   2. Ruling in 1974
      a. Took back most authority given to local community
      b. Local juries did not have "unbridled discretion in determining what is patently offensive"
   3. Summation of current judicial interpretation
      a. Obscenity not protected speech
      b. To rule material obscene, local government must act under laws that specifically define what sexual content is prohibited in words or pictures
      c. Such laws subject to test of constitutionality
      d. Obscenity rules still unclear
   4. Examples
      a. Acceptable legal barriers
         (1) No "kiddie porn" or pornography aimed at children
         (2) No sale of "girly" magazines to minors

(3) Zoning laws to restrict location of "X-rated" theaters and "adult" bookstores
b. Unacceptable legal barriers
(1) Zoning bans on live entertainment to prohibit nude dancing in adult bookstores if bans specifically single out such places
(2) Banning sale of *Playboy, Penthouse,* etc.
(3) Restricting sexually explicit material aimed at adults on the Internet
5. Local effort now more directed at zoning than banning
K. Shield laws
1. No national "shield" laws
2. Some states have shield laws.
3. In the absence of shield law, reporters must reveal sources of information to courts
4. However, Congressional act prohibits searches of "work products" by police unless
a. Persons involved suspected of crime
b. Or material to be seized could prevent death or bodily harm
L. Presence of press at trials
1. Guaranteed on basis of public's right to know
2. Exception when defendant's right to fair trial in jeopardy
3. Does not include right to photograph or televise
4. Some states permit televising

III. Additional Rights
A. Testing for drugs
1. Allowed for public employees
a. Compelling national interest
b. Public safety
2. Drug testing in private sector permitted
B. Prohibition against cruel and unusual punishment
1. Death penalty itself not unconstitutional
2. Court rules for applying death penalty
a. Must not be arbitrary
b. State must prove defendant killed, attempted to kill, or intended that lethal force be used
c. No automatic death penalty
d. No executions of persons under age 18
C. Right to keep and bear arms
1. Second Amendment
2. Historically referred to National Guard, not individual citizens
3. 2008, Court ruled citizens do have right to own guns for hunting and self-protection.
4. However, some restrictions can exist.
D. Right of eminent domain

14th Edition

1. Government's right to take private property for public use
2. Property owner must be justly compensated
3. "Public use" now more broadly defined and controversial
    E. Right to peacefully assemble
        1. Not limited to popular groups
        2. Local officials responsible for keeping peace
        3. Local officials may regulate on content neutral basis
            a. Time of assembly
            b. Place of assembly
            c Manner of assembly
    F. Regulation of sexual acts
        1. Most sexual acts between consenting adults fall into the "zone of privacy"
        2. Government can still regulate some sexual acts
        3. Most states choose not to regulate sexual acts between consenting adults in private
    G. Suicide
        1. Currently illegal
        2. Assisted suicide banned in all states except one
        3. Oregon allows physician-assisted suicide

IV. Limitation on Rights
    A. Listing rights in Bill of Rights might have precluded other rights
    B. Dilemma solved by Ninth Amendment
        1. Listing of rights not complete
        2. Rights may be too numerous to list all
        3. Other rights may come into existence as society changes

Important Terms

Parochial schools
First Amendment
Secular curriculum
Direct Incitement Test
Preferred Position Doctrine
Free Exercise Clause
Establishment Clause
Least Drastic Means Doctrine
Eminent domain
Centrality of political speech
Zone of privacy
Second Amendment

Obscenity
Child Benefit Theory
Shield laws
Equal Access Act
Prior restraint
Slander
Libel
Actionable
Content neutral
Symbolic speech
Political speech
Ninth Amendment

Multiple Choice Questions

Circle the number of the correct answer.

1. The constitutional amendment that deals with freedom of religion, speech, press, and assembly is the

    (1) First Amendment
    (2) Second Amendment
    (3) Fourth Amendment
    (4) Sixth Amendment
    (5) Ninth Amendment.

2. The constitutional amendment that deals with ownership of weapons is the

    (1) First Amendment
    (2) Second Amendment
    (3) Fourth Amendment
    (4) Sixth Amendment
    (5) Ninth Amendment.

3. The constitutional amendment that states that not all the people's rights are contained in the Bill of Rights is the

    (1) First Amendment
    (2) Second Amendment
    (3) Fourth Amendment
    (4) Sixth Amendment
    (5) Ninth Amendment.

4. Congress passed a law making it illegal for police to obtain search warrants for the files and/or pictures in a newspaper or magazine office unless

    (1) national security was being endangered
    (2) the people involved were suspected of a crime
    (3) the material involved had already been published
    (4) the material to be seized could prevent death or bodily harm
    (5) both #2 and #4.

5. The Supreme Court doctrine that holds that the methods used to prevent an illegal action cannot also include legal actions is called the

    (1) Bad Tendency Doctrine
    (2) Least Drastic Means Doctrine
    (3) Clear and Present Danger Doctrine
    (4) Preferred Position Doctrine
    (5) Overbreadth Doctrine.

6. One of the following statements is true. Which one is it?

    (1) Private companies can test employees for drugs only on a limited basis, for example, where the employee might endanger the public.
    (2) Governments may test any employee for drugs merely because these employees are paid by tax dollars.
    (3) Government officials may enforce laws prohibiting sodomy.
    (4) Internet Service Providers (ISPs) must adhere to the rules regarding freedom of speech; therefore, they cannot prohibit material from being sent via e-mail or being posted to Internet sites.
    (5) Local communities may not specifically ban adult entertainment facilities that include nude dancing.

7. The Supreme Court's interpretation of the First Amendment to mean that freedom of speech, press, religion, and assembly should get the highest priority is referred to as

    (1) the Preferred Position Doctrine
    (2) the Fairness Doctrine
    (3) the equal-time rule
    (4) prior restraint
    (5) the centrality of political speech.

8. The Supreme Court has ruled that printed material, among other things, usually may not be censored by government before such material is printed and released to the public. To censor it before release to the public would be referred to as

    (1) the Preferred Position Doctrine
    (2) the Fairness Doctrine
    (3) the equal-time rule
    (4) prior restraint
    (5) the centrality of political speech.

9. The Supreme Court doctrine that holds that criticism of the government is of such importance to a free society that it can almost never be prohibited is referred to as

   (1) the Preferred Position Doctrine
   (2) the Fairness Doctrine
   (3) the equal-time rule
   (4) prior restraint
   (5) the centrality of political speech.

10. Regarding high-school students and their Fourth Amendment rights, the Supreme Court has ruled that

    (1) All students can be required to submit to testing for drug use;
    (2) Only athletes can be required to submit to testing for drug use;
    (3) School officials had to have probable cause and a search warrant to search students.
    (4) School officials could search students without warrants if they believed a crime had taken place.
    (5) Both #2 and #4.

11. The Supreme Court

    (1) Ruled that sexually explicit materials could be banned from the Internet because these materials might be available to minors.
    (2) Struck down a congressional act that, to protect minors, had banned sexually explicit materials on the Internet.
    (3) Ruled against a man who had sent e-mail to a woman in which he discussed kidnapping and assaulting her.
    (4) Refused to allow Internet service providers to prohibit the amount of "junk mail" (a.k.a. "spam") a company could send over its service because such interference violated free speech.
    (5) Ruled that governments may not prevent political candidates from posting signs wherever they want because such action would violate free speech and hinder the democratic process.

12. Suppose the Iowa Medical Association decided to lobby the Iowa state legislature in hopes of getting that body to pass a law prohibiting physicians from advertising except in telephone directories and similar publications. Under what constitutional doctrine might legislators refuse to make such a law?

    (1) Least drastic means
    (2) Content neutrality
    (3) Bad tendency
    (4) Prior restraint
    (5) Clear and present danger.

13. The constitutional doctrine known as the _____ allows the government to punish people who advocate illegal action only if what they are saying or printing is directed to producing such illegal action almost immediately.

    (1) Bad Tendency Doctrine
    (2) Clear and Present Danger Rule
    (3) Least Drastic Means Doctrine
    (4) Direct Incitement Test
    (6) Lemon Test.

Fill-in-the-Blank Questions

Write the appropriate word or words in the blanks provided.

1. Schools that are operated by religious groups are called _____ schools.

2. A school curriculum that includes such typical subjects as language, art, math, biology, chemistry, political science, etc., but does not include the study of religion from an advocacy standpoint is called a _____ curriculum.

3. When prohibiting the distribution of handbills at an intersection, the law must be _____, which means it cannot prohibit distribution of just certain handbills.

4. A type of speech that may involve wearing of some insignia is called _____ speech.

5. The right of the government to take private property for public use is called the right of _____.

6. Laws in some states that protect reporters from having to divulge their sources of information are called _____ laws.

7. Saying things about someone that could ruin his/her reputation or damage that person in some way could be called _____.

8. Writing something about someone that could ruin his/her reputation or damage that person in some was could be called _____ .

9. The _____ Clause of the First Amendment produced many court cases involving freedom of religion and separation of church and state.

10. The Supreme Court has ruled that there is a "zone of _____" into which government may not intrude without very substantial reasons.

11. When the Supreme Court rules that the use of tax money for something connected with parochial-school children does not violate the establishment clause, the Court is using the _____ to interpret the First Amendment.

12. When a controversy is one that can be taken to court, the controversy is said to be _____.

13. That part of the First Amendment that deals with religious *practices* is known as the _____ clause.

14. A group of people who work in the same factory is eating lunch together and talking about a number of current social problems such as juvenile crime. Such conversations would be classified as _____ speech.

True/False Questions

Write the correct answer in the blanks provided.

1. The Supreme Court has ruled that all forms of prayer, whether individual or collective, in the public schools is unconstitutional. _____

2. Posting the Ten Commandments alone on a public-school bulletin board would be unconstitutional. _____

3. If a prayer is nondenominational, it may be recited by students in a public school as part of the school program. _____

4. One-minute periods in public schools for "meditation or voluntary prayer" have been ruled constitutional by the Supreme Court. _____

5. Because legislators, as adults, are not "susceptible to religious indoctrination or peer pressure," according to the Supreme Court, they may open their legislative sessions with prayer and not violate the First Amendment. _____

6. It is constitutional to use tax money to transport parochial-school students to and from school, to buy secular textbooks, to reimburse the schools for tests required by the states, and to reimburse schools for diagnostic hearing and speech tests. _____

7. According to the Supreme Court's current interpretation of the First Amendment, parochial schools from kindergarten through college can receive tax money to construct buildings and to buy equipment as long as the buildings and equipment are not being used for religious purposes. _____

8. Parents of parochial-school children may receive a *federal* income-tax credit for the tuition they paid to send their children to parochial schools. _____

9. The salaries of parochial-school teachers can be paid with tax dollars as long as these instructors teach only such advanced, secular subjects as calculus, not religion. _____

10. Classes, such as comparative religion, may be taught as part of the curriculum in public schools. _____

11. According to the Supreme Court, American citizens have the absolute right to freedom of speech. _____

12. Written or spoken communication may never be prior censored by the government in the United States. _____

13. A law prohibiting advertising by lawyers or dentists might be ruled unconstitutional because it is not "content neutral." _____

14. A law that prohibits door-to-door solicitation by anyone to protect the public against fraudulent collection of money might be ruled unconstitutional on the basis of the Least Drastic Means Doctrine. _____

15. Burning the American flag as a sign of protest is considered by the Court to be protected, symbolic speech. However, burning a draft card is not. _____

16. School rules against wearing the insignia or "colors" of a gang in school would probably be ruled constitutional by the Supreme Court because of the violence associated with gangs. _____

17. People who wish to obtain "conscientious objector" status and, therefore, not be subject to the military draft must be members of pacifist religious groups such as Quakers or Amish. _____

18. Local communities today have tended to move toward control of sexually explicit material by means of zoning laws rather than by prohibiting its sale. _____

19. Reporters are never required to reveal their sources of information if doing so would endanger the lives of their informants. _____

20. Because of the potential for violence, local communities may refuse to allow such groups as Nazis, Communists, or Klansmen to march down the streets under any circumstances. _____

21. Because all sexual practices between consenting adults in private fall under what the Court calls the "zone of privacy," the government has no authority in these matters. _____

22. According to the Supreme Court, public-school teachers may teach remedial subjects in parochial schools without violating the doctrine of separation of church and state. _____

23. The Supreme Court has declared unconstitutional laws against homosexual activity between consenting adults in private. _____

24. The local public high school receives federal money for part of its school lunch program. It recently allowed the local United Way organization to hold a fund raiser in the school's cafeteria. Now the Ku Klux Klan wants to use the cafeteria. The school can refuse the Klan's request because of the potential for violence. _____

25. Because running for political office is covered by the Supreme Court's rulings about the centrality of political speech, a candidate can post signs anywhere without restriction from the government. _____

26. The Church of the Heavenly Trip uses hallucinogenic drugs during its Sunday services so that worshippers may "fly away" to a complete religious experience. The government may not interfere with this practice because it is a religious practice and because it is on private property. _____

27. The government is now regulating all sexually explicit material on the Internet so that children can be protected from seeing this material. _____

14th Edition

28. A conviction for swearing in public is easy to get since all the prosecutor has to prove is that the person actually uttered "swear" words. _____

29. The Supreme Court has ruled that states may not close public schools on Good Friday since that day is a religious holiday. _____

30. Student-led prayer at public-school, sporting events has been ruled constitutional. At such events only prayer led by school officials or clerics would violate the "establishment clause" of the First Amendment. _____

31. The Supreme Court has ruled that obscenity cannot be defined. Therefore, there can be no laws against what is commonly called pornography. _____

32. The Supreme Court stated that reporters must reveal their sources of information to courts and police if called upon to do. _____

33. The Supreme Court has ruled that states cannot prohibit symbolic speech, such as the wearing of black armbands in school. _____

34. The Supreme Court ruled that local juries have a free hand in deciding what was "patently offensive" in sexually explicit material. _____

35. The Supreme Court has decided that official prayers that were read in the public schools were unconstitutional. _____

36. Public officials can easily sue for libel or slander because their actions are protected since they are government officials. _____

37. Because some legal scholars believe the war in Iraq was illegal, law schools were successful in barring military recruiters from their campuses. _____

38. Government employees have no free speech expectations about issues connected with their jobs. _____

39. The Supreme Court has ruled that neither retarded persons nor persons under age 18 can suffer the death penalty. _____

40. According to a Supreme Court ruling in 2008, American citizens have the absolute right to own firearms. _____

41. Because of the dangers of child pornography, persons may not send nude photos of their new babies on a rug, all smiling, over the Internet. _____

Discussion Questions

Use your own paper to answer the following questions.

1. Define the terms *libel* and *slander*. Under what circumstances can a libel or slander case become actionable? Why is it more difficult for public officials to collect damages for libel or slander?

2. Would it be unconstitutional for Congress pass a law prohibiting the possession of firearms by anyone who was not in the military or in law enforcement? Explain.

3. Question #16 in the True/False section asserts that school rules against wearing the insignia or "colors" of a gang in school would probably be considered constitutional by the courts. If you were a lawyer, what argument against such rules could you make using another Supreme Court doctrine?

4. Explain the Supreme Court's interpretation of the First Amendment regarding prayer in public schools.

5. The Supreme Court has been accused of being "wishy-washy" regarding the use of tax money for parochial schools. What rulings has it made that would substantiate this charge?

Using Your Little Gray Cells

1. In the library or through a search on the Internet, you should be able to find a copy of the United Nations document entitled the *Universal Declaration of Human Rights*. How are the Bill of Rights and the UN document alike and how are they different? Is there anything in the UN document that should be adopted by the United States? Why? Is there anything in the UN document that the United States should not adopt? Why?

2. The Ninth Amendment states that the listing of rights in the Bill of Rights should not be construed to mean that those listed are all the people's rights. In light of today's society, what other rights do you think should be included? Why?

3. Give a report to the class about the Supreme Court case *Roe v. Wade* 410 U.S. 113 (1973). Give the facts of the case, the ruling of the Court, and tell whether you agree or disagree with the Court's decision and why? Are your reasons based in constitutional law?

4.   Give a report to the class on the subject of the *Living Will*. Does your state allow living wills? In your opinion is the living will a form of suicide?

5.   In Michigan, a retired pathologist named Jack Kovorkian assisted a number of terminally ill people to commit suicide. Obviously, from his perspective, assisted suicide should be permitted in the law for terminally ill people who choose to die quickly and painlessly. Construct an argument in favor of assisted suicide. When you have finished, construct an argument against it. Which one do you believe should be the basis of any law regarding the matter?

Chapter 18

Equality: Promises and Realities

The real colors of the United
States are white, black, yellow,
And brown.

God took one look at
Adam and brought out
A new model called Eve.

If you put together
Enough minorities,
You have a majority.

Prejudice
Is the Iron Curtain of the mind.

Learning Objectives

After reading and studying the chapter on equality, you should have a better understanding of the following:

1. The meaning of equality;
2. The struggle by minority groups and women for political equality;
3. The constitutional amendments and laws that deal with equality;
4. Devices used to maintain inequality;
5. The difficulties in implementing equality;
6. New emerging minorities;
7. The current status of equality in the United States.

Chapter Outline

I.   Inequality: A Nation Divided
    A.   Americans accept equality as a value
    B.   But disagree on how to achieve it

II.   The Struggle for Political Equality
    A.   The African-American experience
        1.   Freedom Amendments
            a.   Thirteenth Amendment
                (1)   Officially ended slavery in United States
                (2)   1865
            b.   Fourteenth Amendment
                (1)   Granted citizenship to persons born or naturalized in United States
                (2)   States prohibited from limiting or interfering with rights of citizenship
            c.   Fifteenth Amendment
                (1)   States responsible for elections
                (2)   States prohibited from interfering with suffrage because of "race, color, or previous condition of servitude"
        2.   Civil Rights Act of 1875
            a.   Responded to segregation legislation in South
            b.   Prohibited racial discrimination in public accommodations
        3.   The Rise of "Jim Crow"
            a.   Purpose of "Jim Crow" laws
                (1)   Deny blacks' voting rights
                (2)   Segregation of races
            b.   *United States v. Reese*
                (1)   Fifteenth Amendment did not guarantee absolute right to vote

            (2) Guaranteed only against racial discrimination in voting laws
- c. South enacted laws to prevent blacks from voting
  - (1) Literacy tests
  - (2) Grandfather clauses
  - (3) Poll taxes
  - (4) White primaries
- d. *Plessy v. Ferguson* (1896)
  - (1) Separate-but-Equal Doctrine
  - (2) As long as facilities for blacks and whites equal, segregation constitutional

4. Segregation in education
   - a. *Brown v. Board of Education* (1954)
     - (1) Tested Separate-But-Equal Doctrine
     - (2) Actually attacked it on basis of "all men created equal"
     - (3) Court ruled segregation unconstitutional
     - (4) Ordered public schools desegregated
   - b. Compliance difficult
     - (1) Civil Rights Act of 1964
       - (a) Attacked compliance from economic standpoint
       - (b) Cut off aid to schools that did not comply
       - (c) Gave extra aid to schools that did comply
     - (2) South relied on *de jure* segregation, i.e., segregation by law
     - (3) North relied on *de facto* segregation, i.e., North did not prohibit integration by law, but in fact was segregated by housing patterns and intimidation
   - c. Busing used to integrate where other means not successful

5. The ballot
   - a. Black males eligible to vote by Fifteenth Amendment
   - b. But states controlled qualifications despite prohibitions against racially discriminatory laws
   - c. Grandfather clauses declared unconstitutional in 1915
   - d. White primaries declared unconstitutional
   - e. Poll tax declared unconstitutional
     - (1) 1966
     - (2) By court decisions and 24th Amendment
   - f. Civil Rights Act of 1964
     - (1) Limited the use of literacy tests
     - (2) Exempted any voter with sixth-grade education
   - g. Voting Rights Act of 1965: Eliminated literacy tests altogether
   - h. Bilingual ballots
     - (1) Required where "language minorities" exceeded 10% of population
     - (2) 1975

14th edition

       i. Result of changes
          (1) Increased participation in voting by minorities
          (2) Politicians more attentive to minorities
          (3) However, election districts drawn solely on basis of race unconstitutional
6. Public accommodations and facilities
    a. Desegregation by massive demonstrations and media attention
       (1) Led by Martin Luther King, Jr.
          (a) Broke away from NAACP
          (b) Formed Southern Christian Leadership Conference (SCLC)
    b. Civil Rights Act of 1964 effectively eliminated *de dejure* segregation
    c. *De facto* segregation still exists
7. Desegregation of Housing
    a. Devices used to maintain segregation
       (1) Restrictive covenant
          (a) Declared illegal in 1948
          (b) Legal agreements prohibiting homeowners from selling property to minorities
       (2) Blockbusting
          (a) Rumors of blacks moving into neighborhood cause panic selling
          (b) Property purchased cheaply and sold to blacks at profit
          (c) Whites move out leaving neighborhood segregated again
       (3) Realtors steering blacks away from white neighborhoods into black neighborhoods
       (4) Redlining
          (a) Perpetrated by lending institutions and insurance companies
          (b) Refusal to lend money or sell insurance in certain areas because of racial composition
    b. Attempts to integrate housing
       (1) Property owners cannot refuse to sell/rent on basis of race
       (2) Open Housing Act of 1968
          (a) Outlawed blockbusting and redlining
          (b) Banned practice of steering minorities away from white neighborhoods
8. Job discrimination
    a. Civil Rights Act of 1964
       (1) Created Equal Employment Opportunity Commission (EEOC)
          (a) Investigates complaints of job discrimination

14th edition

(b) Attempts to resolve through voluntary means or refers matter to Justice Department for possible legal action

    (2) Employee who claims discrimination must show why a particular practice is discriminatory

   9. Since 1975, income levels of whites declined while those of blacks increased.

  10. Poverty levels of either race still unacceptable

III. Other Minorities in America
  A. Native Americans
    1. Includes American Indians, Eskimos, and Aleuts
    2. Historically Indians particularly abused
      a. Forced to live on reservations initially
      b. General Allotment Act, 1887
        (1) Later called *indigenismo*
        (2) Forcibly removed Indian children from homes and relocated them to government boarding houses
        (3) Perceived as cultural genocide
        (4) Ended in 1934 with passage of Indian Reorganization Act
    3. Attempts by native Americans to bring about change
      a. Demonstrations
        (1) Taking over Alcatraz
        (2) Wounded Knee incident
        (3) Formation of interest group known as American Indian Movement (AIM)
      b. Court action
        (1) Won law suits for millions of dollars because of violations of treaty rights
        (2) Money not enough to offset severity of problems
  B. Asian Americans
    1. Initially suffered much discrimination
    2. Chinese Exclusion Act of 1882
      a. Initially intended to halt Chinese immigration for ten years
      b. Then made permanent
      c. Chinese immigration not unrestricted again till recent changes in immigration laws (c. 1965)
      d. Japanese Americans interned in camps during World War II
      e. Asians overall better off than other minorities in U.S.
      f. History must be judged in context
  C. Arab/Muslim Americans
    1. Balance between security and liberty
    2. 9/11 produced some anti-Muslim attitudes in U.S.
  D. Puerto Ricans
    1. Puerto Rico island territory of United States
    2. No barriers to immigration

3. By 1983, nearly 1/3 of Puerto Rican population migrated to mainland
4. Most have not fared well
5. Gains made at local level mainly
6. F.L.A.N. (*Fuerzas Armadas de Liberacion Nacional*)
   a. Terrorist group with goal of Puerto Rican independence
   b. Question still unresolved

E. Mexican Americans
1. Initially in United States because of conquest or purchase of territory previously held by Mexico
2. Like native Americans, not treated fairly by people or government
3. Became poor, mobile population basically serving agricultural and mining interests
4. Came across border later in barrio programs
5. Now largest minority group
6. Chicano Movement
   a. General name given to civil rights movement for Hispanics
   b. United Farm Workers Organizing Committee
      (1) Led by Cesar Chavez
      (2) Successful in organizing migrant workers
   c. Other groups followed to improve social/economic conditions of Hispanics

IV. Emerging Disadvantaged Groups
A. Examples
1. Gays
2. Elderly
3. Physically handicapped
B. More civil-rights-oriented interest groups in existence now
C. Less money to be divided among more groups
D. Result: fights among groups for smaller piece of budget pie

V. Women
A. Emerging feminism
1. Seneca Falls Convention
   a. July, 1848
   b. Produced the Declaration of Sentiments
      (1) Called for equality for women
      (2) Particularly stressed voting privileges
2. National Woman's Suffrage Association
   a. 1869
   b. Goal: women's right to vote
   c. Achieved in 1920 with 19th Amendment

B. Protectionism and the courts
   1. Laws "protected" women
      a. Alimony and child support
      b. Females given special treatment in working conditions
   2. Also served to protect male position of dominance
   3. *Reed v. Reed*, 1971
      a. Struck down state law that gave males preference in selection of estate administrators
      b. Decision produced others that struck down laws discriminating on basis of sex
      c. Exceptions
         (1) Court upheld requirement of hiring only females as attendants in women's locker rooms
         (2) Court upheld law that does not allow women to be drafted or serve in combat positions in military (Note: This does not mean women cannot be drafted or serve in combat positions. It just means the Court said if Congress wanted to pass a law prohibiting such actions, it could.)
         (3) Fetal protection policies
   4. *Roe v. Wade*, 1972
      a. Established constitutional right of women to abortion-on-demand during 1st trimester of pregnancy
      b. Subsequent decisions declared neither state nor husband could interfere with this right
      c. Met with considerable opposition
         (1) Anti-abortion groups
         (2) Hyde Amendment
            • Prohibits use of federal welfare money for abortion except in certain instances
   5. *Webster v. Reproductive Services*, 1989
      a. Upheld states' right to prohibit state employees from assisting in abortions
      b. Upheld states' right to prohibit abortions from being performed in state facilities
      c. Upheld states' right to require viability test
   6. *Planned Parenthood v. Casey*
      a. If fetus viable, state may regulate or prohibit abortion
      b. *Unless doing so causes "undue burden" on women*
   7. *Gonzales* v. *Carthart, Leroy, et.al.*
      • Upheld Partial Birth Abortion Act, which banned procedure
   8. Equal Rights Amendment (ERA)
      a. "Equality of rights under the law shall not be denied or abridged by the United States or by any state on account of sex"
      b. Split women into basically two camps

                (1) Arguments of STOP ERA principal group to oppose
                    amendment
                    (a) Women would lose special position within legal
                        system
                    (b) Women would be subject to draft and combat
                    (c) Women would lose child support and alimony
                    (d) Women would lose property and pension rights shared
                        with husbands
                    (e) Women would lose maternity leaves and benefits
                (2) Arguments of National Organization for Women (NOW)
                    principal group to support amendment
                    (a) Sex discrimination would legally disappear
                    (b) All women would benefit
                    (c)Denied most claims of STOP ERA
                (3) ERA died June 30, 1982, three states short of passage
      C. Pay differential between men and women
          1. Some attributed to discrimination; remainder to various choices
              women make
          2. Male-dominated and female-dominated occupations
          3. Child care
          4. Feminist proposals for change
              a. Comparable pay
                  (1) Men and women with similar skill levels paid equally
                      even though they hold different positions within
                      company
                  (2) Better day-care facilities--preferably funded at least in
                      part by tax money
                  (3) Improved maternity benefits
                  (4) Shared and flextime jobs
                  (5) Professional-level, part-time positions
              b. Accommodations costly to employers
      D. Politics and contemporary women
          1. Older women's groups concentrated on traditional values and
              concerns of women
              a. Women's Christian Temperance Union
              b. League of Women Voters
          2. New Groups seek "radical' changes
              a. National Organization for Women
              b. Women's Equity Action League
              c. National Women's Political Caucus
          3. Division among and within groups dilutes political power
          4. Some Advances made

VI. Sexual preference
    A. Homosexuals demand equal treatment
    B. "Don't-ask-don't-tell" policy of military

14th edition

C. Boy Scouts could refuse homosexuals admittance

D. Court struck down laws against consensual sex between homosexuals

E. Some states now allow same-sex marriage

VII. Affirmative Action
  A. Justification and use of affirmative action
    1. Discrimination against minorities and women self-sustaining
    2. Direct and positive intervention by government required
  B. Affirmative action plans
    1. Goals
      a. Ideal ratio between minorities and women and white males
      b. Ratio determined primarily by percentage of minorities and women living in area
    2. Measures
      a. Means by which goals to be achieved
      b. Examples
        (1) Deliberate and extensive recruiting
        (2) Preferential treatment of minorities and women in hiring
        (3) Revising selection procedures
        (4) Quotas
    3. Timetable: governmentally established time frame for achieving goals
  C. Criticism of affirmative action
    1. Preferential treatment and quotas should not be used as substitute for hiring based on ability
    2. Produces reverse discrimination
    3. Perpetuates belief in inferiority of minorities and women
  D. Defense of affirmative action
    1. Hiring of unqualified minorities and women not required
      • Requirements must be job-related
    2. Reverse discrimination caused in limited number of instances due to faulty administration of program or interpretation of civil rights laws, not affirmative action itself
      a. Plan must not require that white workers be discharged and replaced with minorities
      b. Plan must not constitute absolute bar to white workers
      c. Plan must be temporary measure
    3. Stereotypes result from attitudes in existence before affirmative action
      a. Tokenism used sometimes to "prove" women and minorities incapable of performing certain jobs
        (1) Hiring unqualified minorities or women
        (2) Failure to give normal assistance
        (3) Placing minorities and women in hostile environment
      b. Most whites oppose affirmative action; most minorities and a minority of women support it

263

Chapter 18

14th edition

E. Challenges to affirmative action
1. *Bakke* v. *Board of Regents of the University of California*
   a. Quotas unconstitutional where whites not allowed to compete for all openings
   b. Preferential treatment on basis of race or sex could be used if employed as positive factor in selection process
   c. Left issues unclear
2. *United Steelworkers v. Weber*
   a. Quotas in this instance deemed constitutional
   b. Bakke case decided by literal interpretation of civil rights laws
   c. Weber case decided by intent of civil rights laws, i.e., to end discrimination
3. Cannot fire longer-term white employees to preserve the jobs of newly hired minorities
4. *Wards Cove Packing Co. v. Antonio*
   a. Disproportionate number of white men not sufficient proof of discrimination
   b. Must prove qualified minorities were passed over because of racial reasons
   c. Burden of proof rests with complainant
5. Challenges to law school reveal a mix of case law.
   a. Race may be used as a factor in admissions
   b. Affirmative action may not be used to remedy past or present injustices.
F. Sexual harassment/discrimination could prove costly to colleges
G. Language battles
H. Correctable disabilities not covered under Americans with Disabilities Act
I. Anti-preferential treatment laws being passed and upheld by courts
K. Affirmative action still "up in the air"
1. Court allows quotas and preferential treatment as long as they do not "unnecessarily trammel" on rights of white males and as long as they are used to correct specific racial or sexual discrimination.
2. Burden of proving discrimination now rests with plaintiff.
3. Quotas may not be used in college admissions

VIII. Summary
A. American ideology includes liberty and equality
B. Divided on how to achieve these ideals
C. U.S. characterized by positives of
1. Freedom
2. Social mobility
3. Overall economic prosperity
D. U.S. still faces difficulties in "refereeing" competing group interests

Important Terms

Voting Rights Act, 1965
Emancipation Proclamation
Fourteenth Amendment
Declaration of Sentiments
Webster v. Reproductive Services
American Indian Movement
Seneca Falls Convention
Separate-But-Equal Doctrine
Brown v. Board of Education
Thirteenth Amendment
Bakke v. California Board of Regents
Martin Luther King, Jr.
Civil Rights Act of 1964
Gonzales v. Carthart, Leroy, et.al.
Open Housing Act of 1968
Planned Parenthood v. Casey
Chinese Exclusion Act
Burlington Northern & Sante Fe RR
  v. White

Fifteenth Amendment
Native Americans
Affirmative action
Partial birth abortion
Grandfather clause
Chicano Movement
White primary
Plessy v. *Ferguson*
Racial gerrymandering
De jure segregation
United Farm Workers
Comparable pay plan
De facto segregation
Restrictive covenant
Voting Rights Act
Hyde Amendment
Nineteenth Amendment

STOP ERA
Blockbusting
Cesar Chavez
Poll tax
F.L.A.N.
Roe v. Wade
Reed v. Reed
ERA
NAACP
NOW
Redlining
SCLC
Tokenism
Jim Crow laws
Literacy test
Viability test

Multiple Choice Questions

Circle the number of the correct answer.

1. The constitutional amendment that granted citizenship to former slaves and prohibited states from interfering with the rights of citizenship was the

    (1) Thirteenth Amendment
    (2) Fourteenth Amendment
    (3) Fifteenth Amendment
    (4) Sixteenth Amendment
    (5) Nineteenth Amendment.

2. The constitutional amendment that officially ended slavery in the United States was the

    (1) Thirteenth Amendment
    (2) Fourteenth Amendment
    (3) Fifteenth Amendment
    (4) Sixteenth Amendment
    (5) Nineteenth Amendment.

14th edition

3.   The constitutional amendment that prohibited the states from interfering with suffrage rights because of race, color, etc., was the

(1) Thirteenth Amendment
(2) Fourteenth Amendment
(3) Fifteenth Amendment
(4) Sixteenth Amendment
(5) Nineteenth Amendment.

4.   The constitutional amendment that granted women the right to vote was the

(1) Thirteenth Amendment
(2) Fourteenth Amendment
(3) Fifteenth Amendment
(4) Sixteenth Amendment
(5) Nineteenth Amendment.

5.   The Supreme Court case in which the Court ruled that separate-but-equal facilities for blacks and whites were constitutional was

(1) Plessy v. Ferguson
(2) Brown v. Board of Education
(3) Smith v. Allwright
(4) Jones v. Mayer
(5) Reed v. Reed.

6.   The Supreme Court case in which the Court ruled that segregation in public schools was unconstitutional was

(1) Plessy v. Ferguson
(2) Brown v. Board of Education
(3) Smith v. Allwright
(4) Jones v. Mayer
(5) Reed v. Reed.

7.   One of the following would be constitutional. Which one?
(1) Preventing women of child-bearing age from working in areas where a hazard to a fetus existed.
(2) Allowing the father of a fetus to prevent the mother from aborting the fetus.
(3) Requiring that potential voters demonstrate the ability to read at the sixth-grade level at least.
(4) Drafting only men into the military.

14th edition

8. The Supreme Court case in which the Court ruled that women had the right to abortion on demand during the first trimester of pregnancy was

   (1) Webster v. Reproductive Services
   (2) Bakke v. California Board of Regents
   (3) Roe v. Wade
   (4) Reed v. Reed
   (5) Smith v. Allwright.

9. The Hyde Amendment

   (1) declared literacy tests illegal
   (2) required a comparable-pay plan for federal-government employees
   (3) established the Griggs Principle
   (4) does not permit federal tax money to be used for abortion except in certain cases
   (5) declared redlining illegal.

10. The Puerto Rican organization that has used violence in its attempts to gain Puerto Rican independence is called

    (1) La Migracion
    (2) the Chicano Movement
    (3) Fuerzas Armadas de Liberacion Nacional
    (4) El Indigenismo
    (5) La Bamba.

11. The Voting Rights Act of 1965
    (1) Gave black people the right to vote in the South
    (2) Required southern states to permit any African American to vote if he/she were eligible by age.
    (3) Banned permanent resident aliens from voting
    (4) Required bilingual ballots in some areas.

12. The term *native American* includes all but one of the following:

    (1) Aleuts
    (2) Eskimos
    (3) All people born in the United States except children of diplomats
    (4) Sioux Indians
    (5) Navajo Indians.

13. The founder of the United Farm Workers Organizing Committee was

    (1) Rev. Al Sharpton
    (2) Cesar Chavez
    (3) Martin Luther King, Jr.
    (4) Phyllis Schlafley
    (5) Jesse Jackson

14. The practice of refusing to lend money for housing or to grant insurance in certain areas because of the racial composition of those areas is referred to as

    (1) blockbusting
    (2) tipping point
    (3) redlining
    (4) the segregation maintenance plan
    (5) restrictive covenant.

15. The Declaration of Sentiments refers to a

    (1) congressional resolution that expressed the United States' intention to acquire territory in the Southwest from Mexico, whether by war or by purchase
    (2) document published by the NAACP and the SCLC that outlined the goals of black Americans in the 1960s in regard to racial equality
    (3) statement issued by American Indians occupying Alcatraz explaining their purpose in taking over the island
    (4) statement drafted by a women's convention calling for equality for women
    (5) declaration by the group known as *Fuerzas Armadas de Liberacion Nacional* expressing its desire for Puerto Rico's independence.

16. A restrictive covenant is a device used

    (1) to set aside a certain number of jobs for minorities or women
    (2) to set aside a certain number of government contracts to minority-owed or women-owned companies
    (3) to prevent racial minorities from voting
    (4) to prevent minorities from buying houses in all-white neighborhoods
    (5) by homosexuals to protect themselves from discrimination.

Fill-in-the-Blank Questions

Write the appropriate word or words in the blanks provided.

1. A _____ was a device used to prevent minorities from voting by requiring them to prove that they could read before they could register to vote.

2. The _____ was a device used in the South to prevent blacks from voting by stating that only whites could vote in the nominating elections.

3. The _____ was a device used in the South to prevent blacks from voting by stating that only people whose relatives had voted before 1867 could vote without passing a literacy test.

4. In the case *Webster v. Reproductive Services*, the Supreme Court ruled that states could require _____ tests before allow abortions to proceed.

5. A device known as the _____ refers to an agreement among property owners not to sell or rent their property to minorities.

6. The _____, a device used to prevent minorities from voting, was outlawed by the 24th Amendment and a number of court decisions.

7. The _____ Act prohibited the immigration of Asians to the United States from the 1880s until well into the 20th century.

8. The pressure group associated with the interests of American Indians is called the _____.

9. In Gonzales v. Carthart, Leroy, et. al., the Supreme Court upheld the congressional act that banned _____

10. Laws that began to appear in the South shortly after Reconstruction had ended and that tended to restrict the freedom of black people are known under the general heading of _____ laws.

11. There are neighborhoods in almost all communities in the United States in which the residents are overwhelmingly, if not completely, from one race or ethnic group. Such residential patterns would be considered _____ segregation.

12. Segregation that results from legal prohibitions against the mixing of races is called _____ segregation.

269
Chapter 18

10. Laws that began to appear in the South shortly after Reconstruction had ended and that tended to restrict the freedom of black people are known under the general heading of _____ laws.

11. There are neighborhoods in almost all communities in the United States in which the residents are overwhelmingly, if not completely, from one race or ethnic group. Such residential patterns would be considered _____ segregation.

12. Segregation that results from legal prohibitions against the mixing of races is called _____ segregation.

13. Segregation of the races, not required by law, which results from such things as housing patterns, is referred to as _____ segregation.

14. The women's interest group that was probably the strongest supporter of the Equal Rights Amendment was the
_____.

15. How many "official" languages does the United States have? _____

16. The _____ Act of _____ (date) did a number of things to end unreasonable discrimination in the United States, including the creation of an agency to cope with job discrimination.

17. The _____ outlawed blockbusting and redlining and banned the practice of steering minorities away from white neighborhoods.

18. The term _____ refers to the hiring of women or minorities merely to say the company hires women and minorities. Companies might even hire unqualified minorities or women or fail to give them normal assistance just to *prove* that women and minorities were unfit for the job.

19. The organization that garnered support to defeat the Equal Rights Amendment was called _____.

True/False Questions

True/False: Write the correct answer in the blanks provided.

1. The Emancipation Proclamation was a statement issued by the women's convention in Seneca Falls, New York, that declared that women should have equal rights, especially the right to vote. _____

270

Chapter 18

14th edition

2.	The National Woman's Suffrage Association was probably the strongest supporter of the ERA in the 1970s and early 1980s. _____

3.	The United Farm Workers Organizing Committee, founded by Cesar Chavez, although appearing to be a farm workers' union, is really a group associated with the Puerto Rican independence movement. _____

4.	As long as facilities for the different races are equal, the Constitution does not prohibit segregation on the basis of race. _____

5.	A business firm has no minority employees. It recruits and hires only one minority so that no one could claim it discriminated. Such behavior would be an example of something we call *tokenism*. _____

6.	According to the Supreme Court's interpretation of the Constitution, Congress may not pass laws to draft only men into the military. _____

7.	Under current laws and court interpretations of the Constitution, there is no way that people who work for the same company in different jobs requiring different skills but similar skill levels can be paid the same. _____

8.	The Twenty-seventh Amendment is known as the Equal Rights Amendment or just the ERA. _____

9.	Once the *Brown* decision was issued by the Court in 1954, *de jure* and *de facto* segregation were ended in the United States. _____

10.	The issue of segregation of the races was really only a regional problem peculiar to the South. _____

11.	A business firm that makes car batteries refuses to allow any women to work in the highest paying jobs at the factory because these jobs involve exposure to chemicals. Such action would be unconstitutional because it denies equal protection of the laws to women. _____

12.	Blockbusting is now an illegal practice in the United States. _____

13.	The use of racial quotas by schools in their admissions policies has been ruled unconstitutional. _____

14.	Native Americans in recent years have received so much money to compensate them for the wrongs done to them in the past that they no longer are considered a disadvantaged minority. _____

14th edition

15. The Chicano Movement refers to the efforts of the city of Chicago to expand into the suburbs. _____ (If you miss this one, you will probably fail this course!)

16. The Supreme Court has ruled that property owners can refuse to sell or rent their property on the basis of race because of property rights in the United States. Private property means you can sell or rent to whomever you please.

    _____

17. Other than discrimination, there are no other factors that could account for the differences in pay between white males and women and some minorities

    _____

18. To make up for past voter discrimination, the Supreme Court agreed that voting districts could be gerrymandered on the basis of race to create majority black or Latino districts.

Discussion Questions

Use your own paper to answer the following questions.

1. How did the attack on segregation in the Supreme Court case *Brown v. Board of Education* differ from that in the case *Plessy v. Ferguson?*

2. How did the main tactic of the NAACP to achieve racial integration differ from the main tactic of the SCLC? What is one possible explanation for the use of different tactics? (Hint: think about the two individuals who led the NAACP and the SCLC during the 1950s and 1960s.)

3. Scratch's Manufacturing Company of Hell, Michigan, maker of smoke detectors, wants to implement an affirmative action plan that would set aside 20% of all jobs in the company for minorities and women. No one else could be considered for these jobs. In addition, female and minority applicants would not be required to show competency for the jobs for which they applied because the company feared it would not be able to reach its quota. The percentage of minorities and women in the town is 5%. (It was a rather warm climate.) Finally, to make up for its past practice of not promoting women and minorities because of racial or sex discrimination, the company's plan aims to promote these employees ahead of white males with more seniority.

   (a) What parts of this plan might be considered legal or constitutional?
   (b) What laws or court cases or principles would you cite to back up your contention that they might be legal or constitutional?

(c)   What parts of this plan might be considered illegal or unconstitutional?

(d)   What laws or court cases or principles would you cite to back up your contention that they might be illegal or unconstitutional?

4.   Why is it difficult for governments in democratic societies to "legislate" equality? Explain.

Using Your Little Gray Cells

1.   Do some research on the event in American history concerning Indians known as the *Trail of Tears*. Present your findings to the class.

2.   Many African American people have last names that were actually the last names of the owners of their ancestors during the slavery period in United States history so as to designate ownership of a human being. Feminists argue that taking the husband's last name upon marriage designates male ownership of females. Construct an argument that women ought to choose their own last names, any name they wish, when they marry.

3.   In the Nineteenth Century, signs could be found in windows and on doors of businesses in such places as Boston, Massachusetts, which had large Irish populations, stating: "No dogs or Irishmen." Do some research into discrimination against the Irish in the United States and present your findings to the class.

4.   In recent years, Asian Americans have been experiencing a new kind of "yellow phobia," which one might call jealousy, because of their generally high academic achievement. Some colleges have set maximum quotas for admittance of people of Asian descent. Give a report to the class concerning this new prejudice based on academic achievement. What solution, if any, do you see?

5.   Phyllis Schlafly was a prominent spokesperson for the STOP ERA movement. Write a report about Ms. Schlafly detailing her arguments against the ERA. Do you agree or disagree with Schlafly's positions? Why?

6.   (a) Explain how the Supreme Court chipped away at the *Roe v. Wade deci-sion* in its *Webster v. Reproductive Services* decision without actually overturning *Roe*. In other words, there were, according to the Court, two

different issues at stake in each of the cases. What were these issues? (b) Write a brief exposition supporting abortion-on-demand, putting forth the arguments you think the most substantial to defend this position. (c) Write a brief exposition supporting a return to abortion being illegal except in cases of rape, incest, and danger to the health of the mother, putting forth the arguments you think the most substantial to defend this position. (d) Can these two positions be reconciled, i.e., is there a compromise position between these two diametrically opposed stances on the issue of abortion? Explain.

NOTES

NOTES

NOTES

NOTES